Adventure Carolinas

ADVENTURE CAROLINAS

Your Go-To Guide for
Multi-Sport Outdoor Recreation

JOE MILLER

The University of North Carolina Press
Chapel Hill

A Southern Gateways Guide
© 2014 The University of North Carolina Press
All rights reserved
Set in The Serif and The Sans
Manufactured in the United States of America

The paper in this book meets the guidelines for permanence and
durability of the Committee on Production Guidelines for Book
Longevity of the Council on Library Resources.

The University of North Carolina Press has been a member of the
Green Press Initiative since 2003.

Library of Congress Cataloging-in-Publication Data
Miller, Joe.
Adventure Carolinas : your go-to guide for multi-sport outdoor
recreation / Joe Miller.
pages cm. — (Southern gateways guides)
ISBN 978-1-4696-1415-1 (hardback)
ISBN 978-1-4696-1416-8 (pbk.)
ISBN 978-1-4696-1417-5 (ebook)
1. Outdoor recreation—North Carolina—Guidebooks.
2. Outdoor recreation—South Carolina—Guidebooks.
3. North Carolina—Guidebooks. 4. South Carolina—Guidebooks.
I. Title.
GV191.42.N72M55 2014
796.509756—dc23
2013041624

Southern Gateways Guide™ is a registered trademark
of the University of North Carolina Press.

18 17 16 15 14   5 4 3 2 1

MIX
Paper from
responsible sources
FSC
www.fsc.org   FSC® C013483

To Elizabeth, Peggy, Ron,
and the other
adventurous souls
who make writing
about adventure possible

Contents

Acknowledgments ix

Introduction: Welcome to a Life of Adventure 1
The Big Six Adventures 3
Ten More Adventures 5
You Can Do It (Yes, You!) 6
How to Use This Book 8
A Word about Risk 10
Without Further Delay . . . 11

Best Destinations by Category 13

Backcountry Exploration 15
What It's About 15
Details, Details 25
Where to Explore 28

Climbing 35
What It's About 35
Details, Details 45
Where to Climb 48
Climbing Gyms 53

Mountain Biking 59
What It's About 59
Details, Details 68
Where to Ride 71

Flat-Water Paddling 81
What It's About 81
Details, Details 90
Where to Paddle Flat Water 95

Whitewater Paddling 103

What It's About 103

Details, Details 112

Where to Paddle Whitewater 117

Scuba Diving 125

What It's About 125

Details, Details 134

Where to Dive 138

Ten More Adventures, in Brief 147

Winter Sports 147

Water Sports 153

Air Sports 156

Land (on Top) 159

Land (Beneath) 159

Acknowledgments

It takes a lot of generous people willing to share their time, expertise, and resources to make a book like this happen. Among those I am most indebted to: Aram Attarian, associate professor of adventure recreation and outdoor leadership at NC State University, a longtime source on climbing and other ways of having fun in the outdoors. Hike leader Steve Martin, who knows that true adventure lies off-trail. The gang at the Triangle Rock Club, including managing partners Andrew Katz and Joel Graybeal, and Mike St. Laurent and Scott Gilliam. Joel especially, for evolving from helpful climbing source to weekly climbing partner. Chris David, who is still exploring strong (while going back to school) in his late sixties and is always willing to share his experiences. Joe Jacob, proprietor of Haw River Canoe & Kayak, my longest-standing and most patient source. Stephen Youngblade, formerly with the National Whitewater Center. Dennis Zullig, my indulgent diving instructor, and Dave Farrar, who along with wife Margie owns Gypsy Divers in Raleigh. Dave has a long history of helping me fulfill my diving dreams. Paul M. Hudy, proprietor of nc-wreckdiving .com, who allowed me to borrow freely from his extensive Web site, which chronicles in fascinating detail the wrecks off the North Carolina coast.

And to all the folks herein who graciously let me tell their stories.

Adventure Carolinas

Introduction
Welcome to a Life of Adventure

Intrigued by the notion of exploring your adventurous side but not sure how to make that happen? With that attitude, you're almost there.

I stepped inside the building, signed a waiver, went into a staging area, got fitted for a harness, rode the elevator to the top floor, walked out into the bright sunlight, took a five-minute tutorial, and then, to my amazement, found myself standing on the edge of the eleven-story building's roof.

I looked to the east and saw downtown Raleigh rising out of the canopy. Then I snuck a quick peek between my legs. I thought I was going to faint.

"You ready?" asked one of the spotters.

"Sure," I replied. And with that I leaned backward out into space.

Scared?

My sweaty hands would have suggested yes. Likewise the wobble in my knees, the quiver in my voice, and the flutter in my stomach as I put my faith in my fellow man and some heavy-duty rappelling equipment.

Yet I had lived through enough similar moments of faith, trust, and adrenaline-jolting adventure to know that I was, most likely, perfectly safe. I'd gone scuba diving on the bottom of the Atlantic. I'd taken up snowboarding at age fifty. I'd gone hang gliding. I'd mountain biked down a black-diamond ski slope. I'd climbed a 600-foot granite dome. And I'd gone kite boarding, or at least attempted to.

And anyone reading this and looking at me would say, "You? Really!?"

Yes, really. Mild-mannered me.

And I'd done it all here in the Carolinas.

The best place to gain a clear perspective on the state of adventure in the Carolinas is from the retail shop at the U.S. National Whitewater

The U.S. National Whitewater Center offers its trademark kayaking and rafting, plus climbing on a 46-foot wall (left) and a zipline that travels above where this photo was taken.

Center in Charlotte. In the back, nestled between the neoprene wet suits, the dry bags, and the river sandals is a floor-length window that looks out on the center's outdoor playground. Dominating the view is the manmade river, a half-mile concrete loop that pumps 12 million gallons of well water over a course that replicates Class II, III, and IV whitewater, suitable for rafts and kayaks alike. To the left is a forty-six-foot-high climbing spire with forty separate routes. A quarter-mile zipline descends from the right. Beyond the tree line to the left is the Catawba River, where kayaks, canoes, stand-up paddleboards, even war canoes capable of toting a dozen paddlers ply the placid waters. Drop your gaze from the canopy to the ground and every few minutes you'll see a mountain biker, a hiker, or a runner emerge from the 17-mile trail network. Canopy tours, eco-trekking, ropes courses—it's all here, too.

THE BIG SIX ADVENTURES

On the 450 acres of the U.S. National Whitewater Center you'll find a microcosm of what the Carolinas has to offer on the adventure front. It's a good jumping-off point for delving into one of the most adventure-friendly regions of the country. Consider:

Hiking, backpacking, and backcountry exploration. With four national forests covering 1.25 million acres and another fifty-nine state parks, lakes, and natural areas covering an additional 184,281 acres—not to mention all other public lands, from national parks to city and county parks to land-trust preserves—there are lots of ways to lose yourself in North Carolina alone. That land mass is multiplied when you take into account the dense foliage and rugged terrain of the southern Appalachians. Consider: a family from Texas visiting Stone Mountain State Park got off-trail and went missing for two days. They were never more than a mile from nearby roads.

Rock climbing. You won't find the multiday pitches of the West and Europe in the southern Appalachians. But you will find an abundance of 400- to 600-foot climbs that offer quality climbing experiences, from top-roping to sport climbing to traditional climbing to bouldering—even ice climbing. There's challenging rock; there's good beginner climbing; and there's lots in between. An abundance of southern exposures makes the region especially popular during the cold winter months.

Mountain biking. Mountain biking may have been conceived on the West Coast, but it quickly found a home in Appalachia. For years, perhaps the most popular mountain biking destination in the country was the Tsali National Recreation Area near Bryson City, its four loops totaling forty miles of trail revered for its flow. Though Tsali still is revered, it may have lost its favored-pedaling status to DuPont State Forest some fifty-five miles east. DuPont boasts nearly one hundred miles of trail and a wide array of riding, including slickrock, the stuff that made Moab, Utah, famous. Say "Pisgah National Forest" and the first thing that comes to many people's minds is stellar mountain biking, and with more than 400 miles of trail, lots of it.

Linville Gorge has been described as the wildest place on the East Coast.

Flat-water paddling. The recreational value of flat water—lakes, marshes, swamps, slow-moving rivers—has only become widely appreciated over the past couple of decades, thanks to the efforts of various tourism and paddling agencies. One of the most successful efforts has been led by the North Carolina Paddle Trails Association, which set out in the mid-1990s to identify and map the myriad trails on black water, marshes, sounds, and small creeks along the coast and coastal plain of North Carolina. In a few short years, they had mapped more than 2,500 miles of paddle trail, making it easy for visitors to the area—as well as locals—to paddle some of the most pristine and scenic waters on the East Coast.

Whitewater paddling. The Nantahala Outdoor Center is the premier training facility in the East. It wasn't by chance that Atlantans Payson and Aurelia Kennedy and Horace Holden Sr. took over the Tote 'n Tarry Motel near Wesser to establish their outdoor center. Not only did the adjoining Nantahala River offer great whitewater, as they'd discovered during frequent vacations, but the location was within a short distance of some of the best and most diverse whitewater in the

Southeast, from the beginner-friendly Tuckasegee to the demanding waters of the Chattooga and Ocoee. Every July, the Carolina Canoe Club bases its popular Week of Rivers festival in nearby Bryson City because of the proximity to rivers that will satisfy both its novice paddlers and its grizzled vets.

Scuba diving. Due in large part to a deadly six-month stretch at the start of World War II, the waters off the Carolinas offer some of the best wreck diving around. German U-boats torpedoed 397 vessels within forty miles of the coast at the start of 1942, creating wrecks that today intrigue more experienced divers (some of the most intriguing wrecks, though, are the few U-boats that were caught in the sights of Coast Guard patrols). Closer to shore beginners hone their skills in shallower waters on wrecks purposefully sunk to create artificial reefs.

TEN MORE ADVENTURES

I singled out the six main pursuits covered in this book because they are either the most popular adventure sports practiced here or because the Carolinas are especially well known for these particular activities. To a lesser degree, I also cover:

- **Skiing and snowboarding.** Thanks to snowmaking, there are six alpine ski areas in the Carolinas (all in North Carolina).

- **Cross-country skiing.** It takes as little as eight inches of snow to set the slats in motion at several popular destinations.

- **Snow tubing.** There are six areas to try tubing, the fastest-growing winter sport in the Southeast.

- **Stand-up paddleboarding.** Born in Hawaii in the mid-twentieth century, the sport was slow to catch on on the mainland but has made up for it of late. You'll find stand-up paddleboarders everywhere from the sounds and surf of the coast to your local municipal lake.

- **Windsurfing.** The Outer Banks is one of the world's top destinations.

- **Kiteboarding.** Windsurfing's brash younger cousin.

- **Hang gliding.** It's been on the wane since the seventies, but still popular at Jockey's Ridge State Park, where anyone with $99 can discover the joy of flight.

- **Ziplines.** A great intro to adventure for folks who may not think they're adventurous.

- **Geocaching.** Especially popular with families.

- **Caving.** Most popular destinations in the Southeast are in states adjoining the Carolinas, but you'll find pockets of enthusiasts here.

That's a lot of opportunities for adventure, and a lot that's new. "There are quite a few things we didn't see five or ten years ago," says Aram Attarian, associate professor in the Department of Parks, Recreation and Tourism Management at NC State University in Raleigh. "Fitness and physical activity have become increasingly important; adventure is just another way of getting out there. And you don't have to be a twenty-something to enjoy it."

Which is one of the main messages of this book.

YOU CAN DO IT (YES, YOU!)

These so-called "adventure sports" are not solely the domain of extreme adrenaline junkies. Sure, they attract the muscled and chiseled, the fearless, those whose physical and mental makeup result from a *Jackass/Nitro Circus*, "Hey, watch this!" mentality. But such folks are the minority. Take mountain bikers. The sport has an image of being dominated by young, male risk takers, a bunch of twenty-somethings riding their bikes off ten-foot drops. Yet according to *Bicycling* magazine, the age of the typical mountain biker in 2009 was thirty-six. Show up for a ride with your local mountain biking club and don't be surprised if at least a third of the riders are female.

Likewise, on one June weekend in 2012 I found the two toughest group hikes I could find, one off-trail at Stone Mountain State Park, the other descending into the rugged Green River Gorge. The majority of hikers on both trips were women. Two in particular, Elizabeth and Peggy, were short on actual backcountry adventure experience but

A diver explores the wreck of the *U-352*. Courtesy of Paul Hudy, nc-wreckdiving.com.

long on backcountry adventure spirit. You can read their stories in the Backcountry Exploration section.

According to the Outdoor Foundation, there were about as many participants age forty-five or older in active outdoor pursuits in 2009 (45.7 million) as there were under twenty-five (46.4 million). In fact, according to the Outdoor Foundation, 39 percent of people forty-five and older participate in outdoor recreation.

In short, this book is aimed primarily at people short on adventure experience, long on the urge to explore. *Adventure Carolinas* gives you a better idea of what these activities are like largely by telling the stories of people who also hadn't pictured themselves as adventurous until they went out and discovered they were.

You may be wondering how this book got narrowed to six main categories and ten subcategories. What deemed these sixteen adventures worthy of inclusion and not, say, trail running or adventure racing, both of which are popular in the Carolinas? Simply put, anything for which competition is the primary reason for being didn't make the cut. Take trail running. I'm an avid trail runner. I love trail running, but without the incentive of a race to train for I would be a less avid, more occasional trail runner. Not everyone who runs trails is that way, but I believe most are. This book is about competition only in the sense of challenging yourself to do more than you think you can. It's not about going up against the guy or gal next to you.

Indeed, "adventure sport" is a squishy term. For a better understanding from which to approach the book, I consulted the aforementioned Aram Attarian, who has specialized in outdoor leadership and adventure education. He's also an accomplished rock climber, paddler, and backcountry explorer. Aram has been enlightening students about outdoor adventure in the classroom since the late 1970s; he's been doing intense field research since well before that. According to Aram, "An adventure sport must involve an element of risk; it must have an uncertain outcome; it must be human powered; and it must have subjective hazards, such as the weather."

The one exception in this book: rock climbing, wherein I include climbing gyms. They qualify on the element of risk and human-powered accounts, and sort of qualify on subjective hazards (a loose bolt on a hold, for instance). As for weather? Well . . . they're a great rainy day alternative, how's that?

HOW TO USE THIS BOOK

Each of the six main sections includes:

A tale of adventure. Want to know what the activity is really like? Let me tell you the stories of the people who do it. People, for the most part, who never considered themselves adventurous, yet were driven to satisfy their curiosity—by going on a "strenuous" off-trail hike, or inadvertently getting into whitewater kayaking, or signing on for a sixty-mile mountain bike race up Mount Mitchell and back. (Yes, I said "race." There is racing in some activities covered herein, such as mountain biking. Racing, however, is not the driving factor for most mountain bikers.)

Venues. Most sections offer twenty or so specific destinations, some close to where you live, some that should be on your adventure bucket

The U.S. National Whitewater Center is known for namesake whitewater, but offers more flat-water options in one spot than you'll find elsewhere.

list. You'll find a synopsis of each area with suggestions on where to go for additional info.

Details, Details. The specifics on how you can get going. Here's a rundown of the information this section covers.

- **Where the activity is done.** A broad view of where the activities can be done in North and South Carolina as well as where they are best done.

- **How to get started.** How do I get my feet wet in a particular adventure sport? Where do I find the people who can teach me what I need to learn? Is taking a class a good idea? If so, where are classes offered? Can I take a class cheap through the local parks and recreation department? What if money is no object and I want an intense immersion class, where can I do that? Is this something I can pick up on my own, maybe with the help of a how-to book or a DVD?

- **Cost.** How much equipment is required? Is it pricey? Can I rent equipment initially? Is used equipment available? Once I buy the basic stuff, am I set for life—or at least until I see something new and shiny? Break it to me: what's it going to cost me?

- **Related associations and organizations.** What are the clubs I should join to meet other aficionados and to stay on top of developments in the sport?

- **Commitment.** Is this something I'm going to have to do a lot to get good at, or can I go out every now and then and still have fun?

- **Physical and mental demands.** Am I going to have to go through the Navy Seal training program in order to physically and mentally handle this?

- **Is it seasonal?** Can I do it year-round or is it only practical certain times of the year?

- **Competitive element.** Are there races or other types of challenges or competitions (e.g., climbing all of the forty-two 6,000-foot peaks in the Southeast)?

- **Folks who do this also tend to . . .** Suggestions for when you've tried, and enjoyed, one particular activity and are ready for your next adventure. Based on surveys and anecdotal evidence.

- **Are the Carolinas a mecca for this activity?** Are North Carolina and/or South Carolina considered one of the best places for this activity?

- **Hot spots elsewhere.** If I like it in the Carolinas, where else can I do it?

- **Resources**

A WORD ABOUT RISK

With anything you do, there is an element of risk. How big that element is rests entirely with you.

Are you prepared for the adventure you are about to undertake? Have you taken a clinic or a lesson? Do you have the proper equipment? Are you going with people you feel comfortable with? Do you have a game plan? For instance, if you're setting out on a backcountry journey in the dead of winter, have you set a turnaround time so you don't get caught out in the dark? And if that should happen, are you carrying a headlamp? If you're doing a river trip, are you going with at least three other boaters? Do you have a throw rope? Extra clothes in a dry bag in case of a mishap?

You control the amount of risk in any adventure. Take the time and you can make rock climbing as safe as lounging in your La-Z-Boy.

WITHOUT FURTHER DELAY . . .

You may have picked up this book thinking you wanted to paddle whitewater, but thumbing through the mountain biking section are suddenly and inexplicably intrigued by the idea of riding a mountain bike up Mount Mitchell. Take some time to read over each adventure in this book. It's difficult to predict how the spirit will strike. Be open.

Then go out and explore.

Best Destinations by Category

With so many great destinations in the Carolinas, how do you narrow the choices? Here are a few ways. (The number in parentheses is the page where the description of the adventure begins.)

Best Beginner Trip

Backcountry Exploration: Stone Mountain State Park (16)
Climbing: Pilot Mountain (51)
Mountain Biking: Forks Area Trail System, Sumter National Forest (78)
Flat-Water Paddling: Merchants Millpond (95)
Whitewater Paddling: Tuckasegee River (121)
Scuba Diving: *Indra* (140)

Best Destination for Intermediates

Backcountry Exploration: Joyce Kilmer–Slickrock Wilderness (31)
Climbing: Rumbling Bald, Hickory Nut Gorge State Park, Lake Lure area (52)
Mountain Biking: W. Kerr Scott Reservoir trail network (74)
Flat-Water Paddling: Edisto River (101)
Whitewater Paddling: Nantahala River (122)
Scuba Diving: *U-352* (141)

Where the Pros Go

Backcountry Exploration: Snowbird Mountains (28)
Climbing: Looking Glass Rock (52)
Mountain Biking: Davidson River area of Pisgah National Forest (76)
Flat-Water Paddling: Folly Island (100)
Whitewater Paddling: Green River Narrows (123)
Scuba Diving: *Papoose* (143)

Best Destination Close to an Urban Area

Backcountry Exploration: Congaree National Park (Columbia) (32)
Climbing: Crowders Mountain (Charlotte) (38)
Mountain Biking: U.S. National Whitewater Center (Charlotte) (73)
Flat-Water Paddling: Congaree River (Columbia) (102)
Whitewater Paddling: Lower Saluda River, Millrace Rapids (Columbia)
    (119)
Scuba Diving: Fantasy Lake Scuba Park (Triangle) (144)

Best Base-Camp Adventure (everything you need out the
    front door of your tent; little or no driving necessary)

Backcountry Exploration: West flank of the Black Mountains (29)
Climbing: Moore's Wall, Hanging Rock State Park (52)
Mountain Biking: Tsali Recreation Area (76)
Flat-Water Paddling: Roanoke River (96)
Whitewater Paddling: Bryson City area (119, 121, 122)
Scuba Diving: Morehead City (140–42)

Backcountry Exploration

It's work to reach the Carolinas' special places, but the payoff is sublime.

WHAT IT'S ABOUT

They were the words I didn't know I'd been waiting to hear, and it took three days of brutal grinding uphill and down to hear them.

"This may be the toughest trip I've ever done," Chris David said as we launched up yet another climb, this one a kick-step affair gaining nearly 1,000 vertical feet in less than a mile. It came at the end of a seventeen-mile day, with thirty-five pounds on my back.

Chris's proclamation carried some weight. He took his first backpacking trip, a fifty-miler, as a Boy Scout in the early 1960s, thru-hiked the Appalachian Trail in 1983, and has pretty much kept going ever since. He's a veteran hike leader for the Sierra Club, and his knowledge of trails in North Carolina's high country is encyclopedic and feet-on, with nearly every mile tromped with about thirty-five pounds on his back. Curiously, though, this forty-two-mile stretch of the North Carolina Bartram Trail had eluded his hiking résumé. This was his virgin run, and he was impressed.

"This may be the toughest trail I've ever done," he repeated in case I hadn't heard him through the kettledrum pounding in my ears.

That you could explore the backcountry of the Carolinas for half a century and still be surprised is no surprise. In the Coastal Plain, dense forest and swampy conditions have long stymied explorers: it took European invaders 300 years after first "discovering" the area to "discover" 16,600-acre Lake Phelps. In the rugged Appalachians, Olympic Park bomber Eric Rudolph eluded capture for five years by hiding out in the rugged Nantahala National Forest around Murphy. Even the supposedly tame state parks aren't all that tame: in 2010 a Texas family became lost for two days when they wandered off a trail at North

Carolina's Stone Mountain State Park. Linville Gorge, a 2,000-foot-deep chasm along the Blue Ridge Escarpment, has been described as the wildest place on the East Coast. There are trails in areas of the Nantahala National Forest that may see only a handful of hikers in a year.

So, yes, it's no surprise that a sixty-seven-year-old outdoor enthusiast such as Chris David is still finding new wild places to explore in North Carolina. The good news is that wild backcountry excursions abound in North Carolina. The better news: you don't have to be a wild person yourself to enjoy them.

Off-Trail at Stone Mountain

On a weekend in the spring of 2012, I set out to explore two of the wildest places I could find. Find, that is, with the help of someone who knew the areas far better than I.

On that Saturday, I tapped into one of "wild and crazy" Steve G. Martin's famous off-trail hikes at Stone Mountain State Park. Since discovering Stone Mountain five years earlier, Steve has made it his mission to uncover every one of the 14,100-acre park's many secrets, very few of which lie along the park's 16.5 miles of blazed and manicured trail. Among other things, Martin has found 350 stills, "Area 15" (a fenced area that may or may not be the entrance to a secret underground military base), and numerous old homesteads previously unknown to park authorities. He has lead about 200 hikes, mostly through the Triad Hiking and Outdoors Group and Triad Hiking Explorers, mostly off-trail, most with such disclaimers as, "If you enjoy nice, marked trails please pick another hike," and, "There's a fifty-fifty chance we won't make it back."

Six of us showed up for this particular hike. We met in a secondary parking lot at Stone Mountain and carpooled to the trailhead. The reason: it would have taken Martin a half hour to explain where the trailhead was, and even then half of us wouldn't have found it. And this wasn't even one of his more challenging hikes. "On a scale of one to ten for calmness," he apologized at the trailhead, "this is probably a three." Calm, perhaps, for wild and crazy Steve. ("Some of my hikes are planned," Steve told us early in the hike. "On our more extreme trips we point to the edge of a cliff and say, 'I wonder what's down there?' and we go.")

Hike leader Steve Martin examines the remains of one of the many stills he's discovered off trail at Stone Mountain State Park.

The morning's hike would follow old, decommissioned trail, long-abandoned roadbeds from Stone Mountain's pre-park days back in the mid-twentieth century, when moonshiners still ruled the region. At least our hike would occasionally follow these long-abandoned road-beds. We'd be hiking for several minutes, then, suddenly, Steve would use his GPS as a divining rod and yell, "Wait! Stop! Two-hundred-and-sixty feet up this hill," and we would dutifully follow him over downed tree trunks, through rhododendron hells, and up the steep rises that characterize the foot of the Blue Ridge Escarpment.

By now, the pack had started to separate. Eileen and Zeddy were at the front, close behind our leader. John was a short distance back. And then, off the back, slowly but steadily plodding along was Elizabeth. Elizabeth wore jeans and sneakers, and stayed in the rear not so much because of the physical challenge but rather, I gathered, to savor the quiet that those of us who stuck close to Martin rarely experienced. She never dropped off the back, and while the hike was obviously challenging her—it was challenging all of us—I never saw her abandon her smile. I was positive she would on one occasion—a swift creek crossing below Lower Falls where the more nimble were able to rock-hop across. Elizabeth eyed the crossing, then slowly began taking off her shoes and socks and rolling up her jeans.

Later, I found out this was Elizabeth's first hike with the Triad Hiking and Outdoors Group. While she hiked some in college, the closest she'd come since was walking her dogs at a park near her Greensboro home. "Why this hike?" I asked. Steve pulls no punches in his hike descriptions; this one was described on the club's Meetup site as moderate/strenuous and included lots of attention-getting red type, capital letters, and exclamation points. In fact, it was the description that *sold* Elizabeth on the hike.

"I liked that it was an easy pace, that the emphasis was on stopping and enjoying," she said. "It's not competitive." Never mind that leisurely and slow is the only way you can approach a hike that eschews the convenience of trails. Elizabeth's goal was to enjoy the natural world. So what if that meant the occasional threat to life and limb.

Descending into the Green River

The following morning I stood in the parking lot of an Ingles grocery on the south side of Asheville, part of a semicircle of Asheville Hiking Group members surrounding our hike leader, Dave. "Any questions?" Dave asked after giving us an overview of the day's hike down into the Green River Narrows.

While I was familiar with Stone Mountain (the part with trails, at least), I had only heard of the Green River Narrows. In fact, I wasn't entirely sure where the Green River was, let alone the "Narrows" for which the Green gets its reputation as an exceptionally challenging hiking and whitewater kayak destination.

A woman bearing a pack suitable for more than just a day hike asked, "How much water should I take? I have a bunch of bottles of water."

Now, if I were Dave I would have made a mental note to keep an eye on this particular hiker, Peggy. The hike was advertised for more experienced hikers, and for good reason: while short (about five miles roundtrip) the trail included a rapid descent into the gorge that included one dizzying section requiring a near rappel. This was a hike that required sturdy hiking boots (*Are those sneakers, Peggy?*) and comfort with rugged, remote locales. Curious about her oversized pack

A dicey descent into the steep Green River Narrows.

and her water-bottle comment, I tossed out the old, "So, you hike here often?" line.

Peggy assured me that this wasn't her first hike with the group. It was her second.

The carpool to the trailhead made me feel better about having no clue where this notoriously wild area was. We drove south on Interstate 26 for a few miles, then headed east on a series of increasingly smaller roads for nearly five miles. The countryside seemed to flatten, and it seemed to be populated in the way much of rural North Carolina is: not densely but consistently. Small houses passed the windshield of our car every eighth of a mile or so. I was just settling in for a long ride when suddenly the lead car in our convoy pulled to the side of the road, and the cars began to empty. I got out and saw a trail disappear into the thick roadside vegetation. But there were no signs of steep mountains that might indicate a nearby 1,000-foot plummet into the earth.

The hike began with a mellow descent on Pulliam Creek Trail, tracing an old roadbed. To reach the Narrows, we had to abandon mellow after less than two miles for a trail that more resembled a quarter-mile-long dirt slide, a slide equipped with a climbing rope, which we all made use of. When we reached the top of this trail, I noticed that the sneakered Peggy had apparently already fallen and scraped her shin and was sporting a nice blood tattoo. About three-quarters of the way down Peggy sprouted a matching cut on the back of her right arm. Jeff, a biology professor at Warren Wilson College, and I stopped to help patch her up.

In the canyon, the trail got rough. What makes the Green River Narrows one of the most challenging whitewater runs in the Southeast are the preponderance of house- and small-apartment-size boulders that the Green—and hikers—must squeeze through, over, and around. This 6.6-mile run has numerous Class IV and V rapids, as well as one Class VI, the notorious Gorilla. Hiking here is a challenge, paddling a matter of life and death. Peggy was in good shape—she told me she does three miles a day on the treadmill—but her sneakers did her no favors. Nor did her oversized pack, nor her asthma. Several of us surreptitiously took turns dropping back and hanging with her, which was no sacrifice because while she acknowledged she was in a little over her head, she was also loving the hike. Later, in fact, as we were slowly making our way out, she told me she was loving her new life, a life that had just begun in Asheville after a thirty-six-year marriage had suddenly and surprisingly ended in Florida. When she arrived back at the trailhead after climbing out of the Narrows, after regaining her breath, she smiled and said, "Thanks to everyone who stayed back and helped me."

Peggy, like Elizabeth the day before, was the least experienced person on the hike. Despite being bruised and bloody, I'm pretty sure she had the best time.

Most Rugged of the Rugged

The North Carolina Bartram Trail was established by the North Carolina Bartram Trail Society to honor naturalist William Bartram, who spent four years (1773–77) exploring the Southeast and documenting the flora and fauna of "the New World." The route (there are Bartram Trails in South Carolina, Georgia, Florida, and Alabama as well) roughly approximates the route Bartram took on his travels (documented in his book, *Bartram's Travels*). It's hard to imagine a trail more emblematic of adventure in the Carolinas than the one taken by a man who dedicated a good portion of his life to understanding what the area was truly about.

Western North Carolina's rugged Nantahala National Forest is as rugged as it gets. Elevations within this half-million-acre forest range from 1,200 feet along the Hiwassee River in Cherokee County to 5,800 feet atop Lone Bald. The forest's very name, Cherokee for "land of the noon day sun," speaks to the region's steep canyons, which only see sun at midday. The more than 600 miles of trail that snake their way through the Nantahala are some of the toughest—and hardest to follow—in the region; the 42 miles on this trip are among the Nantahala's most challenging. Save for an 8.5-mile stretch in the middle, this section of the Bartram Trail is either rising precipitously or dropping so; there are few opportunities to recover. The last six miles, up Ledbetter Creek to 5,049-foot Cheoah Bald, are especially challenging, gaining more than 3,000 vertical feet, much of that over the first four miles.

Chris David and I discovered just how tough the trail was from the start. We had planned to camp the first night at a primitive camping area below Wayah Bald, an eleven-mile hike in from the Wallace Branch trailhead. As it was, we were pressed to reach Locust Tree Gap (the second Locust Tree Gap; there are two within less than five miles), only the second suitable campsite, just before sundown. The relentless climb and the views to the south, made possible by elevation, a crisp winter sky, and a defrocked canopy, conspired to slow our pace.

This is a good time to talk about water, both here and throughout the region's higher climes. If you're doing a day hike in the region's more rugged backcountry areas you might be able to pack enough water in. Even so, you should still come prepared to filter water because few water sources are guaranteed safe from the bacteria, protozoa, and viruses that can live in mountain rivers and streams. Chlorine tablets won't weigh you down (though they take about a half hour to work); the new ultraviolet filters are easy to use (but can be pricey); pumps are fast (if laborious). Always have a backup in the backcountry.

And don't assume there will be water. A pretty standard rule of thumb is that the higher you go, the less likely you are to find water. Springs are common in some areas and generally don't need treating, but they can be hard to find. Some trail maps, especially those produced by the Appalachian Trail Conservancy for the AT, are good about identifying springs. And just because a map indicates there's a stream a mile up the trail, don't assume there will be water in that stream year-round. Even at lower elevations water can be hard to find in summer. Top off when you can.

On this stretch of the Bartram, for instance, water is abundant between miles 21 and 26 and again from 35 to 36.5 (where it follows the Nantahala River). Elsewhere, it's sketchy. For the first 10.1 miles of this trip there was no water. I'd packed in my usual two liters, and thanks to the trail's unexpected challenge had consumed one of those by the time we made camp. Knowing it was another 2.5 miles to water from our current campsite, I decided to forgo my evening tea in favor of morning coffee.

It's a good time to note, too, that of the dozens of decent campsites on this 50.1-mile trip, only five had water. Thus, it's especially important to keep your eye on known water sources and anticipate your water needs. On night two, we pulled into a gorgeous campsite above a waterfall, but the narrow gorge precluded fetching water directly. Rather, we had to walk nearly a third of a mile down the trail to fill up for dinner.

What got my mind off the dearth of water early on were the pristine skies and the promise of 5,342-foot Wayah Bald. "You can see about every mountain in the Southeast," Chris had promised before the trip. Indeed, under winter-crisp clear skies, you could.

Chris David savors a well-earned view from atop Wayah Bald.

From the top of a three-story stone observation tower we looked south to the Standing Indian area, where Chris recounted past journeys on the AT as its summits—Standing Indian, Big Butt, and Albert Mountain—stood crystal clear in profile. We looked west to the Bob Allison area and the Snowbird Mountains beyond. To the northwest we tried to pick out our destination, Cheoah Bald, and to the north we admired the crest of the Great Smokies. Looking back to the east, we tried to figure out which ridges had brought us up from Wallace Branch. The only drawback: Wayah Bald is connected to a picnic area and a 4.5-mile road that brings admiring visitors up from below.

From Wayah, we were looking forward to the 7.4-mile drop down to Nantahala Lake. A nice, mellow descent that would fly by, that would allow for moments of distracted introspection—that would give our legs a break. Some descents in the high country are like that. The generally mellow fourteen-mile return from Clingman's Dome to Fontana Lake, for instance. Or the eight-mile descent from Bluff Mountain in Doughton Park to Basin Creek along Flat Rock Ridge. But not here in the Nantahala National Forest, where descents are marked by sharp drops, quick climbs, and more sharp drops. By the time we reached Nantahala Lake, a three-quarter-mile walk on the shoulder of paved Wayah Road didn't seem so bad. Nor did the six miles that started the next day, along the Nantahala River.

But then it was time for more climbing, up to Rattlesnake Knob (where we inadvertently treed a bobcat), and another knee-jarring descent into the Nantahala Gorge.

The stars of this trip, the features that would be highlighted in the Bartram Trail tourism bureau brochure (if such a thing existed) would be Wayah and Cheoah balds. The postcard moment was the stunningly tough climb up Ledbetter Creek, from the Nantahala Gorge up to Cheoah Bald.

Ledbetter Creek is not big, emptying a very compact drainage. But what it lacks in size it makes up for in ferocity. At the base, where the gorge is too narrow to accommodate a trail and the Bartram detours up—straight up—the side of a mountain, you can hear Ledbetter carving through the gorge a good half mile before rejoining it. In a two-mile stretch mid-climb, it's waterfall after waterfall, culminating in Bartram Falls. Where the 45-degree slopes aren't covered in mountain laurel, rhododendron, and rock outcrops, hardwoods manage to grow sentry straight. Around the four-mile mark a ghost forest inhabits the west slope, the tangle of dead trees testament to some not-so-distant cataclysm. It's take two steps, stop, and gawk.

Just past Bartram Falls, the trail had a change of heart. The narrow gorge gave way to a wide valley. Suddenly, Ledbetter Creek became a passive waterway running through a mellow southern Appalachian hardwood forest. Around mile six there was one more quick, punishing climb before the trail merged near the crest with the Appalachian Trail and, shortly, Cheoah Bald. In clear weather, Cheoah is known for its great views, particularly of the Great Smokies to the northwest. On this occasion, however, the top of the mountain was enveloped in gray. We'd entered the clouds at about 4,700 feet, and by the 5,000-foot mark were in the dead of winter. A light mix of rain and snow was falling along the boreal crest. Rather than feeling threatening, it was cozy.

It reminded me of a year earlier, when I'd climbed Clingman's Dome a month after the road had closed for the season. Hiking through the clouds I suddenly emerged into stark daylight as I hit the empty parking lot. A destination typically jammed with cars and crawling with tourists was abandoned and eerily quiet. I climbed the modernistic observation tower to the top: my only company the distant peaks over 5,500 feet poking through the clouds. I'd hiked ten miles from my backpack base camp and gained more than 4,000 vertical feet. I was tired and still had a ten-mile, 4,000-foot descent ahead of me. But for five minutes I stood and seared the scene—the fluffy white carpet, the protruding blue peaks—into memory.

A backcountry moment, like so many, not soon to be forgotten.

DETAILS, DETAILS

What you need to know to get started in the backcountry.

Where do people explore the backcountry in the Carolinas? As the accompanying list of destinations shows, backcountry adventures exist throughout the Carolinas, from the mountains to the coast. The lush and rugged southern Appalachians may not be as high as the mountains of the western United States, but they're every bit as rugged, and the abundant, nearly junglelike vegetation enhances the effect. With more than a million acres of national forest in North Carolina, there's a lot of room to roam (and get lost in). And as South Carolina shows, you don't need hills for backcountry thrills; the swamps of the Francis Marion National Forest and Congaree National Park present a different sort of backcountry experience. And as hike leader Rod Broadbelt, known for his monthly marathon marches at Raleigh's Umstead State Park, shows in his annual wilderness hike, you don't need a million acres for true adventure; a simple willingness to go off-trail in an urban forest can provide a day's worth of escape.

How to get started. Venturing into the backcountry, especially a backcountry you're unfamiliar with, alone is not a good idea. As our stories show, one of the best ways to explore the trail less traveled (often because there is no trail) is to go on a trip guided by someone familiar with the area. Hiking clubs (find a list at NChikes.com) sometimes do trips to backcountry areas; the Carolina Mountain Club (carolina mountainclub.org) frequently visits such spots. Another good option:

Meetup outdoor and hiking groups. You can find the latter by going to Meetup.com, then searching for "hiking" or "outdoors" groups in your area. One caution: these groups are led by folks like you, only hopefully with more experience. If you're nervous about the hike leader's ability to guide you into—and more important, out of—a backcountry location, send the leader an email and ask about his or her familiarity with the area. If a hike leader hasn't explored the specific area in question at least once, think twice about tagging along.

Is taking a class a good idea? Yes. Even if you're going on a guided hike into one of these wild areas, you should have basic orienteering skills. Orienteering classes are offered through local parks and recreation departments and other outlets, usually for a nominal fee, if any. You'll learn how to read a compass and a topographic map, vital skills for exploring the backcountry. If you plan on spending extended periods in the backcountry, you should also look into a wilderness first-aid course, typically a two-day, eighteen-hour course covering a wide range of potential maladies, from dislocations to shock to head injuries (check the Wilderness First Aid Web site at wfa.net). For more advanced backcountry skills, look into the offerings by the National Outdoor Leadership School (nols.edu).

Cost. If you're already a hiker, chances are you have the basic gear required for an entry-level, one-day backcountry foray: sturdy hiking boots, rain gear, wicking clothes, a well-constructed daypack to store extra clothes (for cold weather, in the event you get wet, etc.), a first-aid kit, and food. Keep in mind, though, that as your backcountry excursions get longer and you explore more rugged territory, you'll be well advised to have higher-quality gear. For instance, say you're used to wearing thin nylon pants on your hikes at the local state park. On a less-well-maintained trail—or off-trail—you'll need thicker pants to withstand the briars, brambles, and rocks you may have to plow through. And because you'll likely be in less accessible areas and out for longer periods of time, you'll want to make sure the gear you've got does what is says it will. Do you really think a $50 jacket can be both waterproof and breathable? Perhaps it's time to part with $300 for the latest in rain technology. The best way to get a gauge on the gear that will best serve you is to consult with folks who are in the backcountry on a regular basis. Outside of transportation, in the case of trips farther afield, once you've got the basics mentioned above you should be good.

Related associations and organizations. As mentioned earlier, it's good to belong to a hiking club. Not everyone in the club may share a penchant for exploring the wildest, most rugged locations, but odds are someone will. Again, find a regional hiking club at NCHikes.com; look into the Carolina Mountain Club (carolinamountainclub.org), as well. And, again, check out the Meetup groups. One group in particular, the Triad Hiking Explorers (www.meetup.com/Triad-Hiking-Explorers) focuses on off-trail hikes.

Commitment. Some activities you need to do regularly to be good at. Not so with exploring the backcountry. As long as you stay in reasonably good shape doing something, there shouldn't be a problem physically if you can only get out every few months.

Physical and mental demands. A moderate-length journey into the backcountry is less taxing than you may think. Why? Because the going tends to be pretty slow. In part, that's because of the obstacles and obstructions you typically have to deal with: a downed hemlock blocking the trail generally requires you to stop and contemplate the safest/sanest way to pass. And, too, the reason you—and your hiking companions, if you have company—are here is for the scenery, the experience. It's hard to take everything in while maintaining a four-mile-per-hour pace. You're likely to be more mentally challenged on such a trip. Things are more likely to go wrong; you're more likely to get lost. Keep in mind one thing: a trip into the backcountry is likely to be far more memorable than a somnambulant hike on a trail you've done twenty times. And remember: it's not a problem, it's a challenge.

Is it seasonal? Depends on the level of adventure you're after. For instance, are you trying to replicate the experience of the first folks to explore what is now South Carolina's Hell Hole Bay Wilderness area, a 2,125-acre coastal swamp? Then, by all means, explore it in summer, when if the ticks and mosquitoes don't get you, the water moccasins and rattlesnakes will. Personally, I'd save Hell Hole for a wintry day when Hell freezes over. Likewise, an area such as western North Carolina's Middle Prong Wilderness has numerous creek crossings; not so bad in the heat of summer, but potentially life threatening in the cold of winter. If you're equipped, mentally as well as physically, go for it. But there's certainly no shame in avoiding the worst of what an already-challenging area has to offer.

Competitive element. With yourself. These are places that few others can or will travel. There's a certain amount of ego in being able to say you've crossed the Black Mountain Crest, the highest ridge on the East Coast, in winter.

Folks who do this also tend to . . . hike and backpack.

Are the Carolinas a mecca for this activity? Plodding through swamps is pretty much the domain of the southeast United States. And while you'll find higher mountains in the West, the southern Appalachians offer a unique challenge posed by dense vegetation, vertiginous mountains, and frequently wet conditions.

Hot spots elsewhere. If you love exploring the Carolinas' backcountry, then any wilderness area will make you happy. Alaska will make you ecstatic.

Resources. See recommendations of groups to hike with.

WHERE TO EXPLORE

Ten places where you're practically guaranteed to get lost.

North Carolina

1. Snowbird Mountains. The more you hear about folks getting lost in the Snowbird Mountains region of the Nantahala National Forest near Robbinsville, the more you want to check it out. Supposedly, there are thirty-seven miles of trail penetrating this rugged area, which also takes in the Unicoi Mountain Range, but it's rare to speak with anyone who's been on actual trail, at least for very long. Advises the National Forest Service map for the region: "Pathfinding is an integral part of the backcountry experience. . . . You will experience the challenge of traveling through these mountains similar to that which confronted the earliest pioneers and settlers." Adding to the area's appeal is the story of one George Mason, who in 1908 got the idea of establishing a 1,600-acre wild-game-hunting preserve in the area for the wealthy. Animals began arriving in 1912, among them buffalo, Russian wild boar, Colorado mule deer, native and Russian brown bear and wild turkeys. However, it wasn't long before the animals began escaping and Mason lost interest in the project. Could Russian brown bears and wild boar still be roaming about? More info: Sherpa Guides, http://www.sherpaguides.com/north_ carolina/mountains/snowbird_mountains/snowbird_area.html. Map: "Snowbird Area Trail Map: Nantahala National Forest," USDA Forest Service, 20-foot contours.

2. West flank of the Black Mountains. Look at a map of Mount Mitchell and the Black Mountains and you see a curious thing. The east flank of the Black Mountain Range is teeming with trails: Mount Mitchell, Colbert Ridge, Woody Ridge, and the Buncombe Horse Range Ridge trails among them. West of the crest? Nothing. It might seem odd to lust after an area with no trails, but I've often stood atop Big Tom or the observation platform on top of Mount Mitchell and wondered, "What's down there?" That curiosity is driven in part by the realization that the west flank is more along the lines of what Elisha Mitchell encountered during his tireless efforts between 1835 and 1857 to accurately measure the height of the mountain that would eventually bear his name. (The waterfall where he fell to his death is on the west flank of the mountain.) Two unpaved roads—one out of the town of Pensacola, one out of Murchison—penetrate the west flank; to the south is a trail network extending from Walker Ridge to Craggy Gardens. More info: Mount Mitchell State Park, http://www .ncparks.gov/Visit/parks/momi/main.php. Maps: "South Toe River, Mount Mitchell & Big Ivy Trail Maps," USDA Forest Service, 1:24,000, 20-foot contours; "Linville Gorge, Mount Mitchell: Pisgah National Forest," Trails Illustrated, 1:65,000, 50-foot contours.

3. Black Mountain Crest Trail in winter. The Black Mountain Crest Trail runs 11.3 miles from Mount Mitchell north down to Bowlens Creek. Many have hiked the rugged spine in summer but few in the winter, when snow (Mount Mitchell averages 104 inches

Backcountry spots in the Carolinas

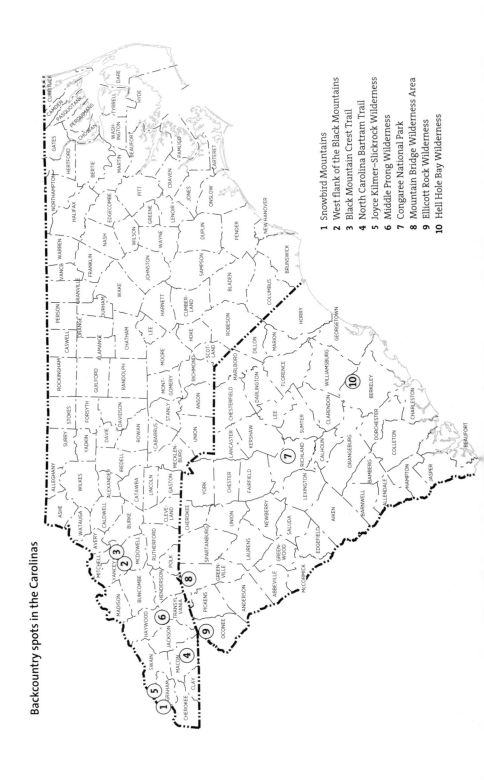

1 Snowbird Mountains
2 West flank of the Black Mountains
3 Black Mountain Crest Trail
4 North Carolina Bartram Trail
5 Joyce Kilmer–Slickrock Wilderness
6 Middle Prong Wilderness
7 Congaree National Park
8 Mountain Bridge Wilderness Area
9 Ellicott Rock Wilderness
10 Hell Hole Bay Wilderness

a year), cold (temperatures have dipped to 34 below zero), and wind (capable of exceeding one hundred miles per hour on the west side) make this a true alpine challenge. Start from the top, at Mount Mitchell State Park, if the roads are clear (and often the Blue Ridge Parkway, which provides the only access to Mitchell, is closed in winter); otherwise, take the 5.5-mile Mount Mitchell Trail up (as in 3,600 vertical feet up) from the Black Mountain Campground. More info: Mount Mitchell State Park, http://www.ncparks.gov/Visit/parks/momi/main.php. Maps: "South Toe River, Mount Mitchell & Big Ivy Trail Maps," USDA Forest Service, 1:24,000, 20-foot contours; "Linville Gorge, Mount Mitchell: Pisgah National Forest," Trails Illustrated, 1:65,000, 50-foot contours.

4. North Carolina Bartram Trail. The good news is that the North Carolina section of the Bartram Trail is, for the most part, easy to follow. The interesting news is that it spends long stretches away from life-nourishing water and never met a hard, long ascent that it didn't prefer to climb straight up. It also includes one of the most physically challenging—and visually rewarding—passages in the state: the six-plus-mile climb up Ledbetter Creek. Steep canyon walls, a ghost forest, an eerie and open high valley near the top, and the payoff atop boreal Cheoah Bald make for a memorable trip. More info: NCHikes.com, http://www.nchikes.com/content/north+carolina+bartram+trail/20835. Map: "An Interpretive Hiking Map of North Carolina's Bartram Trail," North Carolina Bartram Trail Society, 1:35,000, 50-foot contours.

5. Joyce Kilmer–Slickrock Wilderness. One of the most critical trail junctions in North Carolina comes just down the trail from the parking lot at the Joyce Kilmer Memorial Forest. Go left and a bridge takes you over Little Santeetlah Creek into the Disney of old-growth forests; continue straight and you head into the drooling mouth of the 17,394-acre Joyce Kilmer–Slickrock Wilderness. Here, you'll encounter some of the trademark old-growth tulip poplars that bring tourists aplenty to the Joyce Kilmer Memorial Forest. You'll also encounter a wild area guaranteed to keep those same tourists at bay. Take the long hike up to the ridge, then pop over to Slickrock Creek, which bullies its way through a tight, vegetated canyon. Plenty of creek crossings add to the adventure. More info: *Backpacking North Carolina*, by Joe Miller (Chapel Hill: University of North Carolina Press, 2011). Map: Joyce Kilmer–Slickrock Creek Wilderness and Citico Creek Wilderness in the Nantahala and Cherokee National Forests," USDA Forest Service, 1:24,000, 40-foot contours.

6. Middle Prong Wilderness. There's nothing like having a well-known neighbor to keep the masses from adoring you to death. The 7,460-foot Middle Prong Wilderness sits just west and across NC 215 from the better-known Shining Rock Wilderness. Shining Rock gets the lion's share of attention (and foot traffic), while Middle Prong slyly waits to entice those who look at their map and say, "Hey, what's this over here?" Middle Prong is served by the hard-to-find Green Mountain Trail, which takes the high ground following Fork Ridge, the Haywood Gap Trail, which attempts to navigate the drainage by the same name, and the Buckeye Gap Trail, which is something of a middle ground. The wilderness's high ground (it tops out over 6,100 feet) is more successfully serviced by the Mountains-to-Sea Trail. A small wilderness that's big on adventure. More info: NCHikes.com. Map: "Shining Rock & Middle Prong Wilderness: Pisgah National Forest," USDA Forest Service/Southern Region, 1:24,000, 50-foot contours.

South Carolina

7. Congaree National Park. It's hard to imagine a better wild place to explore than a swamp boasting 15,000 acres of primeval forest. Interspersed between those ancient trees—including state record holders and centuries-old bald cypress—you'll find wild pigs, black bears, bobcats, and a variety of rare and exotic birds. You can navigate the park by canoe or, for true adventure, explore the twenty miles of hiking trail that slog through the park. The truly adventurous will be glad to hear there are a handful of camping spots in the swamp, making an overnight stay on a backpack trip possible. More info: Congaree National Park, http://www.nps.gov/cong/index.htm; Wilderness.net, http://www.wilderness.net/NWPS/wildView?WID=134. Map and guides: http://www.nps.gov/cong/planyourvisit/maps.htm

8. Mountain Bridge Wilderness Area. Mountain Bridge is the 11,000-acre area connecting and encompassing Caesars Head and Jones Gap state parks. The area has sections that are rugged and steep—witness the 420-foot Raven Cliff Falls—and while a number of short, less challenging trails attract the masses, much longer and more strenuous trails offer explorers the opportunity to enjoy the region in solitude. More info, including maps: South Carolina State Parks, http://www.southcarolinaparks.com/caesarshead/caesarshead-things.aspx; Hiking the Carolinas, http://hikingthecarolinas.com/mountain_bridge_wilderness.php

9. Ellicott Rock Wilderness. This 8,274-acre wilderness is shared with North Carolina and Georgia, the only wilderness area in the country shared by three states. While man's impact on the land was substantial at one time, that was a good eighty years ago; the lush area is rapidly being reclaimed. One of the true treats of this area is the wild and scenic Chattooga River. This isn't the stretch of *Deliverance* fame (that would be downstream in Georgia); rather, the Chattooga here is less intimidating, more embracing. It's still a rugged hike in, but the trail is relatively easy to follow. More info: Wilderness.net, http://www.wilderness.net/NWPS/wildView?WID=176. Map: USGS, Ellicott Rock Wilderness and additions, South Carolina, North Carolina, and Georgia, 1:48,000, 20-foot contours, 1983.

10. Hell Hole Bay Wilderness. There are four wilderness areas within the coastal Francis Marion National Forest, this one probably carries the most cachet for your adventure résumé. True, that's partly because of the name. But Hell Hole also reeks of what true swamp adventure is all about: venomous water moccasins, copperheads, and rattlesnakes; annoying mosquitoes, chiggers, and ticks; and soggy conditions in all but the driest times of year. But that same hostile environment is what makes 2,125-acre Hell Hole Bay Swamp a good hiding place for endangered species such as the red-cockaded woodpecker. The shallow Hell Hole Canoe Trail affords access by canoe in wet times, by foot when it's dry. More info: Wilderness.net, http://www.wilderness.net/NWPS/wildView?WID=237. Map: USGS, Hell Hole Bay, Wambaw Swamp, Little Wambaw Swamp, and Wambaw Creek Wilderness, South Carolina, 1984.

Climbing

The rugged Appalachians may not be big, but they lend themselves well to climbing.

WHAT IT'S ABOUT

Stuck in the chimney my thoughts flashed back seventeen years to a similar situation. That time I was clinging to the side of a 600-foot granite dome thinking a thought I'd never had in the outdoors: being in an office wouldn't be such a bad thing. An air-conditioned office, behind a desk, both feet planted firmly on solid, cheap, stained carpet. Maybe even with an impossible deadline and an impossible boss looming.

Back in the present, I looked down thirty-five feet to the ground silently seeking direction, but Sarah, our instructor, was talking to another climber. *Why isn't she paying attention to me?* I pouted. Then it occurred to me: she thinks I'm resting, collecting my wits rather than losing them. In the peculiar universe of rock climbing, I was resting. My back was pressed against a rock wall, my legs outstretched, wedged against the rock slab in front of me. I was shaking my arms to relieve the tension and conjure up some lactic acid, trying to get the oxygen back into my bloodstream. Technically, yes, I was resting.

Maybe, but I was also trying to figure out how to get around a small overhang, the crux of this 5.6 climb, and make the last ten-foot push to the top. I tested a couple holds, shuffled my feet, leaned back into the chimney, "relaxed." Around the corner, just to our south in the Three Bears Gully area of Pilot Mountain State Park, a group of community college students from Wytheville, Virginia, were working on their own problem. Another fifty yards up some N.C. State students were climbing the Little Amphitheater. All, I was certain, were making more progress than I.

Two climbers top-rope at Pilot Mountain State Park.

I initiated some movement, which got the attention of Sarah on the other end of the rope. She looked up and watched for a few moments. "Trust your feet," she offered.

Trust your feet. . . . Where had I heard that before?

The Inside Skinny on Outdoor Climbing

The last time I was in such a predicament, that time seventeen years previous, I was a few miles to the northwest at Stone Mountain State Park, and I was a much different climber. In fact, I wasn't a climber at all. It was my first time climbing outdoors, and unlike today I had one big disadvantage: I had virtually no experience in a climbing gym.

Climbing gyms are where more than two-thirds of all climbing is done today, according to the people who track such information at the Outdoor Foundation. And for good reason. Among other things:

- **Gyms are convenient.** You can find them just about anywhere, from converted warehouses to community centers to spiffy, state-of-the-art climbing facilities in towns large and small. (At the end of 2012, there were fourteen climbing gyms in North Carolina, ten in South Carolina.) A decent outdoor climb, on the other hand, can require a day's drive in parts of the Carolinas.

- **Gyms are clear-cut.** Routes are color coded by difficulty; in the great outdoors, while a route may be rated, it is not marked in colored tape. You have to figure out the way up.

- **Gyms are safer.** Ropes and other equipment are tested regularly; in the outdoors, unless you're climbing with a certified and trusted outfitter or have your own gear, it's hard to say how old and worn that rope is you're using.

- **Gyms are contained.** Most climbing gym walls are less than thirty feet high; in the outdoors, a pitch—the distance a typical climbing rope can cover—can approach one hundred feet.

- **Gyms are climate controlled.** Today's gym forecast—and the forecast for every foreseeable day as well—72 degrees and dry.

In a best-case scenario outdoors the temperature will be 72 degrees, the skies clear. Of course, that could change in a moment's time.

As any climber with experience both indoors and out can tell you, experience in the climbing gym is no substitute for climbing outdoors. But then, living in the Carolinas who needs a substitute?

Small Mountains, Big Climbing

"North Carolina's probably got some of the best climbing in the Southeast, along the East Coast, for that matter," says Aram Attarian, associate professor of adventure recreation and outdoor leadership in NC State University's Department of Parks, Recreation and Tourism Management. "It's internationally known."

The state doesn't have the big mountain, multiday pitches common in the West and in Europe: the biggest face in the state is the seven-pitch, 1,100-foot face at Laurel Knob near Sapphire. What it does have is numerous multipitch climbs in the 400-to-600-foot range that offer routes to everyone from beginner to advanced climbers. Especially attractive to beginners, says Attarian, are numerous North Carolina state park venues offering climbing that's "attractive, cheap, and close to home."

Pilot Mountain and Hanging Rock state parks, within a half hour of Winston-Salem and Greensboro, and Crowders Mountain outside Charlotte are good examples. "Pilot is very popular with church groups, schools, and parks and recs," says Attarian. "It's perfect for beginners." In part that's because of the numerous top roping opportunities. This is a good opportunity to pause and discuss the various types of climbing.

- **Traditional.** In the beginning, there was trad climbing, as it is now called. There's you and your climbing gear, and there's a naked mountain. The lead climber makes his way up, setting protection—typically camming devices and nuts that jam into crevasses in the rock and are connected to the climber's rope—as he goes. If you slip, your protection keeps you from falling too far.

- **Sport.** Along about the mid-1980s climbers started installing permanent protection on certain routes. With these permanent bolts, a climber merely had to clip into the existing protection with a "quickdraw" (two carabiners connected with webbing). It made climbing safer and faster in the eyes of some; it diminished the true adventure in the eyes of others.

- **Top roping.** Used on short, one-pitch climbs, this method uses a rope anchored from above. No need for lots of pricey protection and a good intro option for beginning climbers. All reasons Pilot Mountain is a popular destination.

- **Bouldering.** A low-to-the-ground form of climbing, generally done no more than fifteen to eighteen feet off the ground. No protection is needed, other than a crash pad, which the climber hauls backpack style to the boulder and plunks down beneath the climb. You fall, you hit the cushy pad. The fastest growing segment of outdoor climbing because venues are more numerous (you don't need an entire mountain; a small outcrop will do) and the only equipment needed are shoes, chalk, and the aforementioned crash pad.

- **Ice climbing.** Though this style is normally associated with ice-box climates, Attarian says North Carolina "does have good ice climbing—if you know where to look." Spots along the Blue Ridge Parkway shielded from sun (Graveyard Fields, Doughton Park), spots along the roof of the state (Celo Knob, above 6,000 feet on the Black Mountain Crest), even in lower-lying areas, such as the Big Lost Cove Cliffs area of Wilson Creek and Linville Gorge. We are in the South, though, where, Attarian reminds us, "ice climbing has a short window."

While we're taking a narrative time-out, we might as well discuss the difficulty ratings of various climbs, important information to have should a buddy suggest, "Let's go climb Predator at Looking Glass Rock. You're good with a 5.12a, aren't you?"

Climbing in the United States is based on the Yosemite Decimal Rating System and ranges in difficulty from 5.1 to 5.15. Now—

Hold it! Why does the ranking start at 5? What happened to 1, 2, 3, and 4?

Good point. In fact, the Yosemite system does start at 1. Class 1 is an established, flat trail. Class 2 involves a steeper incline; some scrambling may be required. Class 3 is a bit more challenging; you might want to carry a rope, just in case. Class 4 is steeper still.

Class 5 is where things start getting technical—and dangerous. A rope and protection is required. Those Class 5 climbs are broken down as such.

- **5.1–5.4**: Relatively easy climbing, with generous hand and footholds.

- **5.5–5.8**: Holds get smaller; more strength and better technique is required. This is the zone where more casual but well-equipped climbers tend to hang.

- **5.9–5.10**: Where it starts getting challenging. Smaller holds, more vertical faces, possibly an overhang.

- **5.11–5.12**: This zone is reserved for the elite.

- **5.13–5.15**: Beyond elite. Folks who climb in this zone generally spend more time climbing than they do working.

In North Carolina, you'll run into a surprising number of 5.9 and up climbers. For while the North Carolina Division of Parks and Recreation has played a key role in making climbing accessible to beginners, the Carolina Climbers Coalition (CCC) has been instrumental in bringing a range of climbing options into the public fold.

The nonprofit coalition was founded in 1995 to give climbers in the Carolinas a voice. Ten years later it expanded its role by purchasing Laurel Knob, the highest cliff in the East. Laurel Knob has eleven routes, most in the 5.10–5.11 range, appealing to more accomplished climbers. The CCC also brought bouldering to the heart of the Piedmont—at the Asheboro Boulders near Asheboro—and plays a key role in helping to protect the state's other climbing centers.

(Perhaps you've noticed our discussion of climbing opportunities has centered on North Carolina. Although the upcountry of South

Carolina has numerous primo spots for climbing, the activity is only allowed at Table Rock State Park.)

So how do you take that first step toward becoming part of the Carolina climbing community? Let's get back to your feet.

Feets of Strength

... Trust your feet.

I'd heard that phrase before, most recently in the gym, uttered by my climbing partner, Joel. "Don't hug the wall," he'd told me as I hugged the wall while attempting my first 5.9 route. "Lean back and put your weight on your feet. *Trust your feet.*"

But that wasn't the first time I'd heard the phrase. That would have been in an intro to climbing class a few months earlier at the Triangle Rock Club (TRC), an indoor climbing gym in Morrisville, North Carolina.

Intro to climbing classes are less about learning how to climb than they are about learning how to fall. Or rather, how *not* to fall—and if you do fall (and you will), how to fall without bone-breaking repercussions. That's a good thing because once you're assured that it's OK to fall, that you won't break your skull should you part with the wall, your confidence—a key element of climbing—will carry you to new heights. Literally.

That concept quickly became apparent to the seven of us in class. If we didn't have an appreciation for not falling off the wall from twenty feet up at the start, we did after spending the first hour of our two-hour session going over our "protection"—the equipment that would spare us should we part ways with the wall. We started with learning how our climbing harness worked, progressed to putting it on, learned a simple (for some) figure-eight knot, and learned to work our ingeniously straightforward belay device. While we had come to climb, no one complained about spending the first hour on the ground, likely because our balcony classroom overlooked the 9,000 square feet of the gym's climbing surface—a surface from which climbers were routinely dropping only to have their falls arrested by their climbing partners. Mike St. Laurent, our instructor, was in the midst of demonstrating the belay device when we heard a yell—"*Uhhhhhh!*" We turned on our heels in time to catch a fallen climber dangling by his rope.

Mike welcomed the interruption. Each time we heard someone fall behind us, we paid that much more attention to his instruction. Like when he looked at the buckle on his harness and said, "Now if you see the word 'Danger' here, that means you're in danger." We checked our belts for ominous wording as Mike explained that an exposed "Danger" means you haven't doubled the harness's belt back through your buckle. Thus, it's easier for your belt to come undone, which could result in more severe consequences than just your pants falling to the floor. Mike had us practice buckling in once, twice—

"Uhhhhh!"

Most of us buckled in a third time, just to be safe.

Convinced that our harnesses were properly affixed, Mike moved on to communication. Here, he became part climbing instructor, part Dr. Phil. The relationship between climber and belayer had better be one of the best relationships you've got, he told us. None of this, "Your hair looks great with purple streaks, really!" when what you really mean is, "Are you joining the circus?" If something's amiss with your partner's hair, be straight up about it. Likewise, if his figure-eight knot appears to be more of a figure five, or if her belay rope is threaded upside down, speak up. Communication is the foundation of safe climbing.

Before lifting a foot off the ground, the belayer checks the climber's equipment—the figure-eight knot, the harness, with its possible signs of "Danger"—to make sure everything is copacetic. The climber does likewise, checking to make sure the rope is properly threaded through the belay device, the carabiner locked down. After checking one another out, it's time for clearance from the tower.

"On belay?" the climber asks the belayer to make sure the latter is prepared.

"Belay on," the belayer responds, signifying he's ready.

"Climbing," the climber says, seeking final clearance.

"Climb on," the belayer responds, granting permission to ascend.

To our novice eyes, the climbing walls appeared to sport a random scattering of colorful molded polyurethane holds. Some of the holds are whimsical: from faces where the eye sockets and mouth serve as finger holds (or "pockets") to holds shaped like everyday objects such as telephones or light bulbs. Most are simply angular or rounded masses. Some, referred to as "jugs," are big and easy to grab. Some are the smallest of nubs that you can't imagine serving any purpose. As we stared up the wall, though, we noticed that next to nearly all of the holds—and there are perhaps twenty on any one route—was a strip of colored tape. At the bottom, the tape was marked with a number—ranging from 5.5 to 5.13—and a name, sometimes amusing ("Juggy Uppy"), sometimes ominous ("Evil Without"), sometimes head scratching ("Toilet Water"). Looking up the wall we noticed strips of the same colored tape marking certain holds in a pattern of sorts up to the top. Some colors, usually those associated with the bigger, juggier holds, were close together. Others, those marking the smaller holds, seemed far apart. Those related colors, Mike told us, make up routes.

Fortunately, according to Scott Gilliam, TRC's chief route setter, the 110 or so routes up at any one time are divvied up to reflect the climbing expertise of the gym's membership. The Triangle Rock Club has its share of hardcore climbers, but it also has a goodly number of folks not much more advanced than us. Thus, there are plenty of beginner-friendly routes in the 5.5, 5.6, and 5.7 range. "I try to peak around 5.9 and 5.10," Scott said. "You won't find many 5.13s."

No one in our class was out of shape. In fact, everyone was active in some other pursuit: running, cycling, triathlon. And while that's no doubt an advantage, it also becomes clear on our first climb that you don't have to be a wiry athlete to be a recreational climber.

"If you can climb a ladder, you can climb," says TRC managing partner Joel Graybeal.

Our forays up two 5.5 routes were surprisingly easy, their ease ensured by following one key piece of advice: it's not your arms that count, it's your feet. Your initial inclination, especially as you get farther from the ground, is to cling to the wall. That, we quickly discovered, quickly zaps your arm strength. Rather, put your weight directly over your feet, which requires that you ease your body back from the wall. Counterintuitive and a bit disconcerting at first, but natural once you get the hang of it.

Trust your feet!

We scampered up the twenty-five-foot wall, and while I later learned that a great training exercise is to downclimb the route you went up, it was time for another lesson from Dr. Phil, this one about trust. Once at the top, it's time to let your partner get some experience catching you and lowering you to the ground. That required letting go of the wall. Again, from twenty-five feet up. But before that can happen, some more open communication.

"Take!" yells the climber, informing her belayer that she would like to be gently lowered to earth.

"Gotcha!" yells back the belayer, which in climbing parlance means, "I've got you. Trust me."

In my climbing so far, that had proven to be true

Meanwhile Back in the Chimney

Back in the chimney at Pilot Mountain, I scooted my feet down until each was perched on precariously slim lips of rock. Then I pulled myself forward and up with the help of a pair of substantial hand holds. I'd reached this point a few minutes earlier. Now was the time to trust my feet as my hands sought less substantive grips above and to my right. I reached with my right hand for a small gripper while gingerly shifting weight to my right foot. Then, seemingly on their own, my left foot and leg brilliantly decided they would best serve the cause by wedging against the wall that, moments earlier, my back had been pressed up against. The pressure on my right foot eased. The tiny crimpers my hands pinched suddenly seemed like hearty jugs. I used my feet to inch up another foot, found much better hand holds, hoisted myself up another foot, made a series of quick moves and topped out.

"Nice!" came a yell from below.

I'd done climbs rated up to 5.9 in difficulty in the gym. This was a mere 5.6. Yet it was indoor apples vs. outdoor oranges, fanciful colored urethane molds vs. Mother Nature's gritty monochromatic granite. Stuck in that chimney I had to figure out on my own how to get out, up, and over. There was no colored tape to lead the way.

An outdoor world of difference. Yet the lessons learned in the gym —the mental lessons, the essential need to believe in yourself and your feet—translated well.

DETAILS, DETAILS

What you need to know to get started climbing.

Where do people climb in the Carolinas? Primarily in the mountains, almost exclusively in North Carolina (legally, at least). While the high country of South Carolina has a number of attractive possibilities, access issues have so far kept all but one of them locked up. In North Carolina, there are a number of popular hot spots, including the Hickory Nut Gorge Area, Linville Gorge, and the Panthertown area. You'll find legitimate climbing as far east as Pilot Mountain State Park and Hanging Rock State Park, and bouldering in the Asheboro area. That's outdoor climbing. In both states, there are climbing gyms from coast to mountains, including ten in South Carolina and fifteen in North Carolina. See related lists of outdoor destinations and climbing gyms in both states.

How to get started. "Find a mentor, someone experienced, someone willing to work with you," advises NC State's Aram Attarian. Among your options for places to find such a mentor are climbing gyms, colleges, guide services, parks and recreation departments, and Meetup groups. "There are so many more options than there were when I started climbing thirty years ago," says Attarian.

Despite the differences between indoor and outdoor climbing, the best place to start for either activity is probably an indoor gym. Many of the same principles and techniques that apply to outdoor climbing apply in the gym as well. It's a more economical way to test the waters, and it should give you a sense of whether clinging to a precarious perch well above the ground is something you're interested in pursuing.

Is taking a class a good idea? It is the only idea. Climbing is a safe sport, provided you know what you're doing, and there is a lot to know about this activity, from how to tie a knot to how to break your partner's fall. Climbing gyms offer instruction, often for free or for a nominal charge in the hopes you'll become a regular. Full day introductory group classes generally start around $75 per person.

Cost. Indoor climbing is cheap to try. For $15 at most gyms, you can rent the basic equipment—climbing shoes, harness, and chalkbag—

as well as a day's worth of gym time (you and your arms will be lucky your first time out to last more than an hour). Some gyms even throw in a beginning climbing class for free or for a modest fee. Testing the waters outdoors will be more expensive. One of the cheapest ways to try outdoor climbing is through intro programs offered by a growing number of parks and recreation departments. Such courses generally start around $100 and include equipment, transportation, and instruction. Beginner instruction through a private service will generally cost two to three times that amount for a two-day class.

That's to get your foot in the door. Once you're inside and like what you see, expect to pay a minimum of $100 for climbing shoes—and, yes, you do need these specialized shoes. Their tight fit and hard rubber edges are the difference between you saying, "Man, I did a 5.8 route my third time out!" and "Climbing sucks." If you find that bouldering is your thing, you'll only need to spring roughly another $20 for chalk and a chalk bag. (If you plan to boulder outdoors, plan to spend another $140 or so on a portable crash pad.) If you're planning to confine your climbing to a gym, you'll need to spring for a membership or a punch card. Rates vary, but $50 a month is a good membership baseline. You'll also need a harness ($50) and belay device ($15–20). If you plan to climb outdoors, you'll need additional equipment. You'll need a rope regardless of what form of outdoor climbing you plan to do; expect to pay in the neighborhood of $150 for a basic sixty-meter rope. You'll need a helmet ($60) and, if you plan on traditional climbing, a quiver of protection devices. This is where climbing can get expensive. Simple nuts can run $10 or so; more involved camming devices can cost $60 and up. Considering a typical pitch may require at least a dozen pieces of protection, it's easy to see how the cost can add up.

Related associations and organizations. The Carolina Climbers Coalition (carolinaclimbers.org) is the regional advocate for climbing in the Carolinas. The CCC plays a vital role in gaining access to the region's top climbing spots, both in terms of advocacy and in the outright buying of land. Most recently, the CCC has been involved in securing climbing and bouldering at Laurel Knob and Rumbling Bald and in Asheboro. Annual membership is $20.

Various Meetup groups throughout the Carolinas offer climbers a chance to meet and climb. Outdoor Club South has chapters in various cities in the Carolinas, and there are numerous climbing-specific Meetups throughout the region. Go to Meetup.com and search based on "climbing" and your zip code.

Commitment. As a climber at the Triangle Rock Club once told me, you climb once a week to maintain, twice a week to get better. Strength and technique are equal partners in the climbing world, and both need attention if you are to advance in this sport.

Physical and mental demands. First, the physical. There's a widely held belief that you need to be a solid muscle in order to climb. As is the case with the elite of any sport, that is true if you want to pioneer 5.15 routes in Yosemite. But here's the secret to most climbing: while hand and arm strength are certainly helpful, smart climbers let their legs do a majority of the work. Center your weight over your legs, and let your legs power you up the wall as much as possible. Practice good technique and climbs up to 5.9 should be within the grasp of anyone in moderately good shape. Remember, as Joel Graybeal of the Triangle Rock Club says, "If you can climb a ladder, you can climb."

Climbing is much more about the mental. With traditional climbing in particular, but also in the climbing gym, much of successfully getting up a face or wall involves solving problems—which is why they call routes "problems." You must figure out the most feasible way to get up the wall, then convince yourself that you can do it. Successful climbing requires an intense focus, which is part of why avid climbers consider the activity such a great escape: when you're climbing, you can't afford to spend mental energy fretting over life's assorted challenges.

Is it seasonal? One of the region's big advantages is that you can climb *somewhere* year-round. Rock faces whose southern exposure makes them uncomfortable to climb in summer, for instance, make ideal venues come winter. Likewise, those northern faces that are too cold in winter (save for ice climbing, perhaps) are perfect for the heat of summer. Climbing gyms, of course, are year-round.

Competitive element. Most of the competition in rock climbing is internal: you're constantly challenging yourself to try more difficult routes. There are, however, competitions for the more externally competitive. Odds are your local gym sponsors at least one competition a year. Probably the most well-known climbing competition in these parts is the Triple Crown Bouldering Series (triplecrownbouldering.com). As its name implies, the annual series consists of three events, held in the fall, at Hound Ears in Boone, N.C.; Stone Fort in Chattanooga, Tenn.; and Horse Pens in Steele, Ala.

Folks who do this also tend to . . . dabble in other adrenaline sports. Two particularly popular side pursuits for climbers are mountain biking and trail running.

Are the Carolinas a mecca for this activity? "North Carolina's probably got some of the best climbing in the Southeast, along the East Coast, for that matter," says NC State's Aram Attarian. Because of the state's milder climate and abundance of rock faces with southern exposure — the Rumbling Bald area of North Carolina's Hickory Nut Gorge, for instance — the state is particularly popular as a winter destination.

Hot spots elsewhere. Good climbing exists anywhere worldwide where you have mountains. On the East Coast, the Shawangunks — or "Gunks" to the devout — in New York State are popular. In the West, great climbing abounds, from Eldorado Canyon outside Boulder, Colo., to the epicenter of U.S. climbing at Yosemite National Park in California. Then there's Europe, the birthplace of mountaineering and climbing.

Resources. AshevilleNow.com, http://www.ashevillenow.com/outdoor -activities/rock-climbing/; Carolina Climbers Coalition, http://caro linaclimbers.org; SummitPost.org, http://www.summitpost.org; Rock Climbing.com, http://www.rockclimbing.com/routes/North_America/ United_States/North_Carolina/Western/

WHERE TO CLIMB

From state parks to national forests to spots rescued by the Carolina Climbers Coalition, North Carolina is rife with places to climb. Here's a look at where to climb by type of climbing, with the degree of difficulty at each site. Note: bouldering is rated on a scale of V0 (easiest) to V16 (crazy hard).

North Carolina

BOULDERING

1. Asheboro Boulders, Asheboro (V0–V5). Popular bouldering area for Piedmont climbers. Located on private property, with access made possible by the Carolina Climbers Coalition. Terms of the lease call for climbers to be members of the CCC. More info: Carolina Climbers Coalition, http://carolinaclimbers.org/climbing-areas/asheboro boulders/asheboro-boulders.html

2. Dixon School Boulders aka Buzzard's Roost, Crowders Mountain State Park, Kings Mountain (V2–V7). Longtime bouldering venue recently embraced by North Carolina State Parks with the help of the Carolina Climbers Coalition. More info: Rockclimbing.com, http://www.rockclimbing.com/routes/North_America/United_States/North_Carolina/Western/Dixon_School_Boulders/

3. The Dump aka Warpin Endorphins, Blowing Rock (V0–V5). Plenty of challenging sport and top-rope climbs in addition to bouldering. More info: Rockclimbing.com, http://www.rockclimbing.com/routes/North_America/United_States/North_Carolina/Western/The_Dump_aka_Warpin_Endorphins/

4. Hound Ears, Boone (V0+) More than 200 "problems" make this boulder compound highly popular—for one day a year. That would be on the date of the annual Hound Ears Bouldering Competition (part of the Triple Crown), the only day this area in a gated community is open to climbers. More info: Rockclimbing.com, http://www.rockclimbing.com/routes/North_America/United_States/North_Carolina/Western/Hound_Ears/

5. Moore's Wall, Hanging Rock State Park, Danbury (V4–V8). For more info, see number 15 below.

6. Rumbling Bald, Chimney Rock (V3–V8). For more info, see number 13 below.

Climbing and bouldering spots in North Carolina

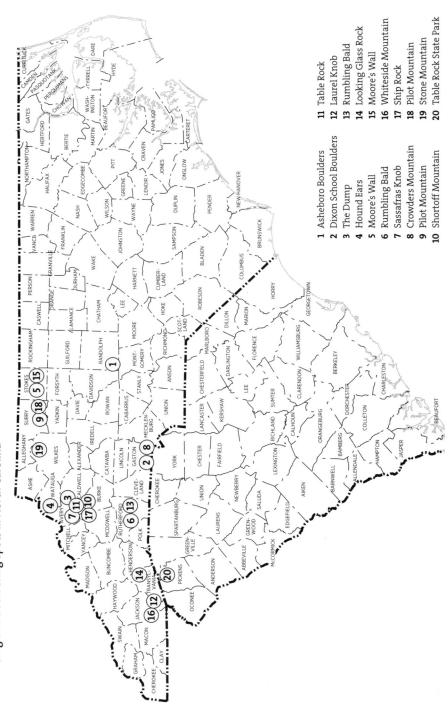

1 Asheboro Boulders
2 Dixon School Boulders
3 The Dump
4 Hound Ears
5 Moore's Wall
6 Rumbling Bald
7 Sassafras Knob
8 Crowders Mountain
9 Pilot Mountain
10 Shortoff Mountain

11 Table Rock
12 Laurel Knob
13 Rumbling Bald
14 Looking Glass Rock
15 Moore's Wall
16 Whiteside Mountain
17 Ship Rock
18 Pilot Mountain
19 Stone Mountain
20 Table Rock State Park

7. Sassafras Knob, Pineola. The Vortex route is 17 feet high with a V10 rating. More info: MountainZone.com, http://www.mountainzone .com/mountains/detail.asp?fid=1507356

SPORT

8. Crowders Mountain, Crowders Mountain State Park, Kings Mountain (5.7–5.13). Easy access, close to Charlotte. There are 40 routes listed in *Selected Climbs in North Carolina*, by Yon Lambert and Harrison Shull (Seattle: Mountaineers Books, 2002), and as many as 140 routes reported elsewhere online. More info: Rockclimbing.com, http://www.rockclimbing.com/routes/North_America/ United_States/North_Carolina/Western/Crowders_Mountain/

9. Pilot Mountain, Pilot Mountain State Park, Pinnacle (5.5–5.12). Easy access, proximity to Piedmont population centers (the Triad and Triangle), and good variety of sport and traditional routes make this one of the state's top crags. Open exposure and lower altitude make Pilot especially attractive in winter. More info: Carolina Climbers Coalition, http://carolinaclimbers.org/climbing-areas/pilot -mountain.html

TRADITIONAL (TRAD)

10. Shortoff Mountain, Linville Gorge, Linville (5.6–5.12). Linville Gorge offers a range of good climbing opportunities; this may be the best. Located at the southern end of the gorge, Shortoff offers some of Linville's longest routes, and challenging access keeps the crowds down. More info: AshevilleNow.com, http://www.ashevillenow.com/ outdoor-activities/rock-climbing/

11. Table Rock, Linville Gorge, Linville (5.4–5.12). Considered some of the best beginner and intermediate climbing in the state, Table Rock includes several multipitch 5.5 and 5.6 bolted routes. Some routes can be top roped. More info: AshevilleNow.com, http:// www.ashevillenow.com/outdoor-activities/rock-climbing/ wnc-rock-climbing-spots/#whitesides

12. Laurel Knob, Panthertown Valley area, Sapphire (5.8–5.11). Highest cliff in the East at 1,100 feet. Features slab and water-groove climbing.

Says the Carolina Climbers Coalition, "If you like classic traditional NC climbing and haven't yet been to Laurel, you need to get out there at least once." More info: Carolina Climbers Coalition, http://carolina climbers.org/climbing-areas/laurel-knob/laurel-knob.html

13. Rumbling Bald, Hickory Nut Gorge State Park, Lake Lure area (5.7–5.12). Southern exposure has long made this one of the most popular winter climbing destinations in the country. The range of climbing and bouldering opportunities can cause crowds. More info: Carolina Climbers Coalition, http://carolinaclimbers.org/climbing-areas/rumbling-bald/rumbling-bald.html

14. Looking Glass Rock, Davidson River area near Brevard (5.6–5.13a). Possibly the state's best-known climbing destination. 500-foot white granite dome offers seemingly endless variety of climbing opportunities. Some bouldering as well. More info: AshevilleNow.com, http://www.ashevillenow.com/outdoor-activities/rock-climbing/

15. Moore's Wall, Hanging Rock State Park, Danbury (5.5–5.13). Cliffs running 400 feet in height and extending nearly two miles offer a variety of climbing opportunities. Includes Cook's Wall, also popular, though access is via private land. More info: North Carolina State Parks, http://www.ncparks.gov/Visit/parks/haro/activities.php; Mountain Project, http://www.mountainproject.com/v/moores-wall/105932741

16. Whiteside Mountain, Pisgah National Forest, Highlands (5.9–5.12c). Boasting some of the highest cliffs in the East, Whiteside has a variety of climbing opportunities and a rarity for this part of the country: a ten-pitch climb of more than 750 feet. More info: SummitPost.org, http://www.summitpost.org/whiteside-mountain/152974#chapter_2

17. Ship Rock, Milepost 303, Blue Ridge Parkway (Rough Ridge parking area) (5.6–5.13a). Another North Carolina must, Ship Rock has good access (and thus, can get crowded) and is a good destination in spring, summer, and fall. More info: AshevilleNow.com, http://www.ashevillenow.com/outdoor-activities/rock-climbing/

18. Pilot Mountain. For info see number 9 above.

19. Stone Mountain, Stone Mountain State Park, Traphill (5.5–5.12). It's mostly friction climbing up this sloped, 600-foot granite dome, which climbers say defies easy description. Says AshevilleNow.com: "if scary runouts on slab, not knowing when you might slide down the cheese grater, sounds like fun to you . . . Stone Mountain is the place to be." More info: AshevilleNow.com, http://www.asheville now.com/outdoor-activities/rock-climbing/

South Carolina

20. Table Rock, Table Rock State Park, Pickens County (5.9-5.12). South Carolina's only legal climbing area, the climbing surface of Table Rock is a 350-foot granite face visible from SC 11. Climbing is restricted to August through December, with the best weather in November and December.

CLIMBING GYMS

Don't have time to head to the mountains? Chances are there's a climbing gym or wall near you. Here's a list of twenty-four walls throughout the Carolinas.

North Carolina

MOUNTAINS

Asheville

Asheville's Fun Depot
7 Roberts Road; 828-277-2386
http://www.ashevillesfundepot.com
24-foot wall

ClimbMax Inc.
43 Wall St.; 828-252-9996
http://www.climbmaxnc.com

Unlike in the great outdoors, the routes are named and color coded at your neighborhood climbing gym.

Montford Climbing Wall

34 Pearson Drive; 828-253-3714

http://www.ashevillenc.gov

12 top-roped routes

Boone

Footsloggers

139 S Depot St.; 828-262-5111

http://www.footsloggers.com

Outdoor, 40-foot tower

Brevard

Brevard Rock Gym

224 South Broad St.; 828-884-ROCK

http://brevardrockgym.com/

Charlotte

Inner Peaks Climbing Center
9535 Monroe Road, Suite 170; 704-844-6677
http://www.innerpeaks.com/
13,000 square feet of climbing space

U.S. National Whitewater Center
5000 Whitewater Center Parkway; 704-391-3900
http://usnwc.org
Outdoor tower, 46 feet high

Triangle

Chapel Hill Community Center
102 South Estes Dr., Chapel Hill; 919-968-2790
http://www.townofchapelhill.org/
20 routes, limited hours

Triangle Rock Club
102 Pheasant Wood Ct., Morrisville; 919-463-7825
http://trianglerockclub.com/
24,000 square feet of climbing space, 50-foot wall, free-
    standing 14-foot high bouldering area

Triangle Rock Club–North Raleigh
6022 Duraleigh Road, Raleigh, 919-803-5534
http://www.trianglerockclub.com/temp/trc-north-raleigh/
13,100 square feet of climbing space, 30-foot freestanding
pillar, 16-foot-high bouldering area

Triad

Tumblebees Ultimate Climbing Gym
6904 Downwind Road, Greensboro; 336-665-0662
http://www.theultimateclimbinggym.com/
40-foot walls

Fayetteville

RedPoint Indoor Climbing
5213 Raeford Road, Suite 103; 910-868-7625
http://www.redpointgym.com/
8,000 square feet of climbing space

The Climbing Place
436 West Russell St.; 910-486-9638
http://www.theclimbingplace.com/
18,000 square feet of climbing space

COAST

Jungle Rapids
5320 Oleander Dr., Wilmington; 910-791-0666
www.junglerapids.com
30-foot wall

South Carolina

UPCOUNTRY

Trailhead Climbing & Outdoor Center
505 Camson Road, Anderson; 864-225-1010
https://sites.google.com/site/trailheadclimbingcenter/
50-foot-high climbing walls, more than 6,500 square feet of
   wall space

Glendale Outdoor Leadership School
270 Wheeling Circle, Glendale; 864-529-0259
http://setgols.org/Indoor-Rock-Climbing.html
20- to 25-foot walls, two bouldering areas, 1,000 square
   feet of climbing wall

The Mountain Goat
61 Byrdland Dr., Greenville; 864-469-5048
http://www.mountaingoatclimbing.com
25-foot walls

Climb Upstate
208 Daniel Morgan Ave., Spartanburg; 864-699-9967
http://www.climbupstate.com
Climbing wall and bouldering cave

Climb@Blue Ridge
301 Bulls Road, Taylors; 864-895-1416
www.climbbr.com

MIDLANDS

Stronghold Athletic Club
925–1/2 Huger St., Columbia; 803-256-9001
http://www.facebook.com/pages/
    Stronghold-Athletic-Club/117199188299444
6,000 square feet of climbing space with 40 foot walls;
    leading/top roping.

Greenwood Family YMCA
1760 Calhoun Rd., Greenwood; 864-223-9622
www.greenwoodymca.org
>30-foot climbing wall with two auto belays

LOW COUNTRY

Goose Creek Community Center Climbing Wall
519-A N. Goose Creek Blvd., Goose Creek; 843-569-4242
http://www.goosecreekrecreation.com/
30-foot indoor wall, 3 auto belay devices.

Charleston

Coastal Climbing
708 King St.; 843-789-3265
http://www.coastalclimbing.com/
1,600 square feet of bouldering surface

The Climbing Wall
James Island County Park; 871 Riverland Dr.; 843-795-4386
http://www.ccprc.com
50-foot wall, 4,500 square feet of climbing space, 1000-
    square-foot bouldering cave

Mountain Biking

You don't even need mountains to do it.

WHAT IT'S ABOUT

It begins innocently enough, with a graduation present you didn't know you wanted, or with the realization that it's the only cardio exercise that keeps your interest for more than ten minutes, or when you suddenly and unexpectedly find yourself in the middle of a race. One thing leads to another and before you know it, you're pushing your bike up a 5,000-foot peak in a raging thunderstorm swearing you'll never ride a mountain bike again—*ever*!

That is, until three hours later when the skies have cleared and you're wondering how soon the trail will dry out so you can do it all over again.

Mountain biking may be the most addictive of the adventure sports in the Carolinas. One day you're straddling a borrowed bike, peering nervously down a narrow dirt trail that disappears into the woods, thinking, *This is nuts! No way can I squeeze through those trees.* And before long . . . you're clipped into your own bike, a carbon fiber marvel of technology that cost more than your car, picking a line through a steep rock garden in the Pisgah National Forest.

Crazy.

Mountain biking may have been birthed in the foothills of Marin County, California, in the early 1970s (though if you've seen *Butch Cassidy and the Sundance Kid* you may think Paul Newman got things rolling some seventy years earlier), but it was made for the southeastern United States. A mountain bike's fat, knobby tires are ideal for rolling over tree roots and rocks; the suspension systems are built to absorb the punishment of rugged terrain; the gearing—we're up to thirty gears and counting—is designed to handle the steepest climbs. Roots and rock, rugged terrain, steep climbs—if that doesn't say southern Appalachians, I don't know what does.

In the early days of the sport's boom, in the early 1990s, western North Carolina's Tsali Recreation Area, with four sweeping loops accounting for forty miles of trail, was considered the top destination in the East. In some riders' eyes, it has since been supplanted—by another western North Carolina destination, DuPont State Forest, which has nearly one hundred miles of trail, including some rare (in the East, anyway) slickrock, a feature that makes western locales such as Moab, Utah, such popular worldwide destinations. Western North Carolina's Pisgah National Forest, and its Pisgah District in particular, has hundreds of miles of single track, the narrow natural-surface trail preferred by mountain bikers. Meanwhile, across the state line in South Carolina, the twenty-five-mile Forks Area Trail System in Sumter National Forest gives newer riders a place to ride for hours on end.

In 2011, *Outside* magazine named the Pisgah National Forest one of the top five mountain biking destinations in the United States. "Losing yourself in the hundreds of miles of mountain biking trails in the vast, million-acre Pisgah, which surrounds Asheville, North Carolina, is the fun part," gushed the magazine. "Finding your way back to the car before dark is the challenge." (Which is why, after you're addicted, you'll think nothing of paying $600 for a 1400 lumen headlamp that'll light the forest brighter than a high school football stadium on Friday night.) *Outside* is particularly smitten with the Bent Creek, Davidson River, and Mills River areas.

When Singletracks.com asked its readers to rank their favorite mountain bike trails in 2013, seven from North Carolina made the list: Tsali Recreation Area (at number 5), Dupont State Forest (12), Warrior Creek (26), Dark Mountain (35), Overmountain Victory Trail (38), Bent Creek (44) and Wild Turkey (60).

The International Mountain Bicycle Association's "bucket list" of mind-blowing trails includes nine in the Southeast. One of those nine, the Forks Area Trail System in South Carolina's Sumter National Forest, hosted the annual IMBA World Mountain Bike Summit in 2010.

In both states, good riding cascades down from the high country into the more populated Piedmont. North Carolina boasts sizable trail networks in the Uwharrie National Forest, the Wake County parks sys-

A popular element of mountain biking is the night ride.

tem, and Greensboro's watershed lakes trails, while South Carolina's Midlands region has ten networks with at least ten miles of trail each. Ironically, even *coastal* areas of the Carolinas offer opportunities for *mountain* biking—in North Carolina, at Bicycle Post in Greenville and Blue Clay in Wilmington, and on more than thirty miles of trail in South Carolina's Charleston County.

Great beginner spots near where we live, some of the most challenging terrain in the country in the southern Appalachians. It doesn't get much better than that.

Sure, you say, for testosterone-infused twenty-something single guys for whom *Jackass* and *Nitro Circus* are not spectacle but lifestyle.

Not really.

The myth of mountain biking doesn't mesh with the numbers. According to the National Sporting Goods Association, 6 million Americans mountain biked in 2011. More than 36 percent were female, and the mean age of a mountain biker was about thirty-two. That latter number may surprise anyone who's been to a mountain bike race, where the majority of racers are in their thirties and forties, and there's usually a goodly number of riders who score a seniors discount down at the K&W after the race.

At the 2012 Off Road Assault on Mount Mitchell, for instance, of the 397 racers who finished (480 started) the sixty-three-mile mountain race with 11,000 total feet of climbing, only 26 were under thirty, meaning 93 percent of the riders were over thirty, and 46 percent were over forty.

Youngsters? In their own minds, perhaps, but not in the eyes of the U.S. Census Bureau.

So who exactly are these people, these mountain bikers?

The Biker Dudette

Melissa Cooper would take issue with the adrenaline-crazed biker dude stereotype.

When Cooper graduated from Campbell University in 2008, her dad gave her a mountain bike for graduation, a gift she didn't know she wanted. At first, Cooper rode the bike on short errands around Durham, where she had moved to attend grad school at Duke. Then someone suggested she try the dirt trails at nearby Umstead State Park and Lake Crabtree County Park. "I liked it," says Cooper.

Before long, she was riding all the local Triangle trails and began entering local cross-country competitions and six-hour endurance races. She liked those, too, so when a friend said he was planning to sign up for ORAMM, that led to the obvious question:

ORAMM?

Races, such as the Off Road Assault on Mount Mitchell, which begins in Old Fort, are a part of the mountain biking culture.

It stands for Off Road Assault on Mount Mitchell, an annual sixty-three-mile mountain bike race that begins and ends in Old Fort and in between climbs a total of 11,000 vertical feet into the Black Mountains. It's one of numerous mountain bike races that might have you thinking, *Me? Ha!*

You might want to think again, though.

To be sure, events such as ORAMM, PMBAR (Pisgah Mountain Bike Adventure Race), Double Dare, the Pisgah 111K, Swank 65, and others attract a goodly number of über-fit adrenaline junkies. But such events also represent a logical progression for the everyday rider who suddenly finds him- or herself a devotee of the fat tire. At ORAMM 2012, for instance, Jeremiah Bishop, a pro racer for Cannondale Factory Racing, crossed the finish not long after noon, in a record time of four hours, thirty-three minutes, and sixteen seconds. Only 17 more racers would finish within the next hour. Seventy percent of the field (276 racers) would take seven hours or more; 47 percent (185) would take more than eight hours; and 7 racers would spend more than twelve hours on the course, finishing after sunset.

The vast majority of the pack had no chance of reaching the podium, even in their age group. Sure, they were competitive, just not with Jeremiah Bishop. With themselves.

So why were they out there?

"I couldn't get over how pretty it was, looking around at the mountains, off in the distance," says Cooper of her first ORAMM. Indeed, while much of the rock-and-root-infested undulating single track demanded focus and didn't leave much room for sightseeing à la the Blue Ridge Parkway, there were long stretches of tame, if sometimes steep, Forest Service road that did allow riders to take in the waterfalls on Curtis Creek, the mature southern Appalachian hardwood forest blanketing the east flank of the Black Mountain range, and the occasional bear that wandered across the route.

That must be some impressive scenery to bring Cooper back after her first run at ORAMM in 2010.

"I was at the highest elevation of the race, pushing my bike up to the top of Heartbreak Ridge and then starting downhill in the middle of heavy rain, dark clouds, thunder, and lightning," Cooper recalls of ORAMM 2010. "When you're on a bike at the top of a mountain, streaks of cloud-to-ground lightning, followed immediately by deafening thunder, are a very good incentive to try to descend . . . as fast as possible!"

The Family Man

Daniel Hemp would take exception to the image of mountain biker as daredevil goof, too. With two kids and a construction business to run, Hemp can hardly put his health in jeopardy. Which is why, curiously, he got into mountain biking.

Hemp's is a familiar story: active through college ("I played lacrosse all my life"), he graduated, got married, and started building a business. A decade passed, two children were added to the mix, and suddenly, in his mid-thirties, Hemp realized he was no longer fit.

"I wasn't overweight—I have a high metabolism," says Hemp. "I just wasn't in shape."

One day Hemp found himself and his bike at Lees-McRae College, just out for a casual ride, nothing special. Lees-McRae is home to one of the more high-profile collegiate mountain bike teams in the country, and he noticed a bunch of bikers in their kits were gathered. As Hemp took in the scene, the school's coach walked over.

"You racing?" the coach asked.

"Sure," said Hemp, forking over the $10 entry fee.

"It was a short-track race, a three-quarter-mile loop through the woods. It lasted, like, twenty minutes, and I was hooked.

"I could never get a workout like that on my own," Hemp says of trying to keep pace with the younger riders. "I could never sustain 170 [heart] beats per minute on my own."

He continued showing up for the weekly races and within the next two years went on to do several of the more notable mountain bike races in the region (Iron Mountain 100K, Burn 24 Hour Challenge, Icycle)—and eventually to invest in a higher-end bike and cosponsor his own bike team.

The Bone Doctor

And there's Jason Leonard. If there's anyone who might be suspicious about the perceived dangers of a bone-rattling mountain bike ride, it would be Leonard, a chiropractor.

Like Daniel Hemp, Leonard was in his mid-thirties and searching for a better way to stay fit.

"I was a gym-goer, three days a week," recalls Leonard. "For cardio, fifteen minutes on the treadmill was a crazy workout for me."

He knew he needed something more to benefit his heart. "I wanted to do a marathon," he says. "I got to six miles, then ten miles, and I said, 'You know what? I don't want to run any farther.'"

Then he heard about mountain bike "marathons" and thought he'd give that a try.

He was in chiropractic school in Charlotte at the time and had the good fortune to stumble upon the popular trail at Colonel Francis Beatty Park. The seven-mile trail is geared toward beginners, and judging from most of the comments on mountain bike Web sites, it's been responsible for luring more than one mountain biker into the fold. The trail is known for being flat with nice flow and good, if not big, jumps.

"I thought it was pretty cool," says Leonard. "It was completely different from anything I'd ever done. You have to work hard, but it's fun enough to make you enjoy it."

And, in Leonard's case, to lose upwards of forty pounds.

Mountain? You Don't Need No Stinkin' Mountain.

Melissa Cooper's and Jason Leonard's examples underscore what may be the true allure of mountain biking in the Southeast. Sure, we've got killer trail worthy of national acclaim in the mountains. But we've also got great networks in lower climes near where the majority of Carolinians live. Maybe you don't have time to drive to Bent Creek for the weekend. But you probably can squeeze in a morning ride in town.

A quick rundown, first in North Carolina:

Charlotte offers the aforementioned Francis Beatty Park as well as the seventeen-mile trail network at the U.S. National Whitewater Center. The latter is tailor-made for beginners, a well-marked system where the easy trails are clearly distinguished from the not so easy (stay on the green, avoid the blue, and if you find yourself on a black with a name such as "Toilet Bowl," get off and call 911). And it's one of the few places where you can rent a bike (as part of the admission) and take a spin in the same location. If you like it, continue to ride; if not, take your bike back and go rafting, or climbing, or ziplining . . .

The Triangle has beginner trail spread throughout the region, but probably the most popular starter trail is at Lake Crabtree County Park in Morrisville. Lake Crabtree was the first legal single track in the Triangle, opening in 1992, and though it has expanded and replaced existing trail it has remained true to its beginner roots.

The Triad offers lots of beginner options at the venerable Country Park, Horizon Park, and Tanglewood, among other areas.

Greenville. I was always surprised by how many good mountain bikers from Greenville showed up at mountain bike races—until I rode the Bicycle Post trails on the northwest side of town. Miles of trail on a compact piece of private property offer a surprising number of options for greenhorns.

Wilmington. You might think a coastal port city would be happy to have just one mountain bike trail network, but Wilmington has three! Blue Clay and the Burlington Nature Park offer more varied terrain, while the trails on the University of North Carolina Wilmington are ideal for beginners, with lots of flowing single track threading the pines.

And in South Carolina:

Charleston. With a national forest—Francis Marion—in your backyard, the odds are good you'll have some decent trail. But more than fifty miles worth, most of which, owing to its coastal location, is super beginner friendly?

Columbia. The multiuse (meaning you'll share the trail with hikers and equestrians), three-mile Stewardship Trail at Harbison State Forest and the 6.1-mile Sesqui Trail at Sesquicentennial State Park both offer good options for beginners.

And the previously mentioned Forks Area Trail System—known by its entirely appropriate acronym, FATS—offers thirty miles of mostly beginner-friendly trail in southern South Carolina, near Augusta, Georgia.

For the uninitiated, "fats" is shorthand for "fat tires," referring to the fat—or fatter, at least, than the skinny tires on a road bike—tires that make rolling through the forest possible. It's an apt moniker, and a reminder that, in the Southeast, good opportunities for riding can be found just about anywhere—in the Piedmont and at the coast, as well as in the mountains.

It's a sport for all terrain, and for all people.

Other Mountain Biking Options

So far, we've been talking about the most common and popular form of mountain biking, cross-country. There are at least two other types of mountain biking popular in the region.

Downhill. This more extreme version of the sport involves heavy-duty bikes run over trails that head down steep hills. (In fact, the beefier downhill bikes can weigh—and cost—twice as much as their cross-country counterparts.) Because of the downhill nature of the sport, it's generally found as a summer option at ski areas. North Carolina's Beech Mountain, for instance, has downhill trail on its slopes that are served by the resort's ski lifts. Bike rentals typically include a full-face helmet and body armor—which should tell you something about what lies ahead.

Pump track. A more recent development in the mountain biking world, pump tracks are short courses—typically measured in yards rather than miles—that cleverly employ tight, bermed turns and humps. The goal is to build enough speed that, by shifting your weight and manipulating your bike you can make it around the pump track without having to pedal. Works better on rigid bikes and bikes designed specifically for pump-track riding. One of the top pump tracks in the Carolinas is the Riverview Pump Track in North Augusta, South Carolina.

DETAILS, DETAILS

What you need to know to get started mountain biking.

Where do people mountain bike in the Carolinas? Everywhere. While it certainly is true that mountain biking is done in the mountains—and that's where more seasoned riders prefer to ride—there are numerous trail networks in and near every population center throughout the Carolinas. (See "Where to Ride")

How to get started. First, obviously, you need a mountain bike. Buying one represents a significant investment in something you're not sure you'll like. So what are the best ways to test-ride the sport? You have three options.

1. **Rent.** Many bike stores rent mountain bikes. Most rent middling bikes that are serviceable and will give you a good feel for riding. Some rent higher-end bikes in the hopes that the plush ride will be more likely to suck you in. Expect to pay $50 to $100, depending upon how sophisticated the bike is, for a twenty-four hour rental. Some stores will apply your rental fee toward the purchase price of a bike should you decide to buy.

2. **Demo day.** Check with your local bike shops and see when their next demo day is scheduled. The bigger bike manufacturers bring vans of their new bikes to local trail networks

and let riders take them out for a spin. Most demo days feature a good cross section of bikes; if you know going in that your budget is $800, then ask to ride a bike in that range. Warning: test ride a pricey, sophisticated bike and you will be spoiled. Upside to the demo day: this is a no-cost option. Downside: you may have to wait a while before a demo rolls into town.

3. **U.S. National Whitewater Center.** A day pass to the U.S. National Whitewater Center in Charlotte ($54 as of 2013) gets you in the gate and gives you access to fifteen activities, including mountain biking. Check out a bike, take it for a spin on their seventeen miles of single track (there's lots of beginner-friendly trail), and if you like it, swell. If not, you can still go whitewater rafting, or climbing, or ziplining, or stand-up paddleboarding, or . . .

If, after taking a test ride you decide you're in, hook up with a local bike club or mountain biking Meetup group. Almost all hold periodic (monthly, usually) beginner rides led by more experienced riders who are more than happy to share their expertise and give you tips.

Cost. Mountain biking isn't cheap, but after the initial investment—your bike—your biggest expense will be transportation. About that initial investment, the first and most important decision is where to buy. Keep in mind two things: stuff will go wrong with your bike (stuff that you will need to get fixed), and you probably know little about mountain bikes. Thus, it behooves you to deal with someone who really knows bikes. Buy your bike from a local bike store, and when things go wrong you can take it in and get it tweaked or fixed, often free of charge (most bike stores include a free comprehensive one-year care package). It's important to get a bike that fits, and most bike shop employees can help with that. If you hit the trail and the bike doesn't feel quite right, you should be able to take it back and get the shop to adjust it—again, for free. The second thing: when you tell the folks at the bike shop that your budget is $150 and they start laughing, don't be offended. Most bike shop employees aren't on commission and they aren't in the business for the big bucks; they're in it because they love bikes and they want you to love bikes, too. Even if they had a $150 bike on the floor, they likely wouldn't sell it to you. A decent front-suspension bike will run you at least $600; a full suspension closer to $1,200 and up. Some bike shops have trade-ins that you can pick up cheaper. For kids' bikes, an increasing number of stores have trade-up programs that offer generous trade-in allowances. As a result, these stores are generally stocked with less expensive used kids' bikes. Other expenses: immediately, you'll want a hydration system (starting around $50) and a spare tube, basic tool kit, and pump ($25 and up). Before long, you'll find yourself lusting after the more expensive stuff: clipless pedals, bike shoes, a cycling computer, and on and on. Mountain Bike World offers a good online guide to how to buy a mountain bike: http://www.mountain-bike-world.com/buy-a-mountain-bike/.

Related associations and organizations. In the Southeast, most bike clubs are affiliated with SORBA—the Southern Off-Road Bicycle Association (www.sorba.org/)—which is affiliated with IMBA—the International Mountain Bicycle Association (http://www.imba.com/). You can find your local SORBA chapter at their Web site.

Commitment. I quit playing golf years ago because I had to play twice a week just to maintain my sorry handicap. This is not so much the case with mountain biking: once you attain a certain level of technical skill, it tends to stick. However, don't expect to go out every six months and ride thirty miles of single track. Aerobically, you will be doomed.

Physical and mental demands. Obviously, if you ride in the mountains and are doing a five-mile trail that gains 3,000 vertical feet, this sport will be physically demanding. Riding the rolling and flat portions of the Carolinas, not so much. Because so many of our trails in the Southeast are rocky and rooty, focus is important. You are constantly assessing a variety of obstacles.

Is it seasonal? The main natural constraint is rain. Most public trails close under wet conditions to prevent erosion and trail degradation.

Competitive element. Nearly every trail system in the region is home to at least one race a year, and nearly every population center has some sort of race series. Charlotte, for instance, has the Charlotte Mountain Bike Series, which offers a cross-country race every Wednesday evening at different locations around town from April into September.

Folks who do this also tend to . . . dabble in other adrenaline sports. A particularly popular sidelight of mountain bikers is hitting the climbing gym.

Are the Carolinas a mecca for this activity? Tsali in the Nantahala National Forest; Bent Creek, Davidson River, and Mills River in the Pisgah National Forest; and DuPont State Forest all have national reputations. (See "Where to Ride" for details.)

Hot spots elsewhere. Ready to devote your vacations to mountain biking? Go West, young fat-tire fanatic. Moab, Utah; Fruita, Colorado; and Sedona, Arizona, are among the most popular U.S. destinations.

Resources. Charlotte Mountain Bike, www.charlottemtnbike.com; Tarheel TrailBlazers, www.tarheeltrailblazers.com; Greensboro Fat Tire Society, greensborofattire.org; Mountain Biking in the Triad, www.mountainbikethetriad.com/;Singletracks.com;Triadmtb,http://www.singletracks.com/mountain-bike/metroMap.php?page=NC+Triad; TriangleMTB.com; Triangle Off-Road Cyclists, torc-nc.org; MTB WNC, www.mtbikewnc.com; Pisgah Area SORBA, http://www.pisgaharea sorba.org/; Singletracks.com, www.singletracks.com; Sir Bikes-a-lot, sirbikesalot.com; Cape Fear SORBA (Southeastern Off Road Bicycle Association), capefearsorba.com; Down East Cyclists, downeastcyclists.com; Midlands SORBA, http://www.facebook.com/MidlandsSORBA; South Carolina State Trails Program, sctrails.net; Singletracks.com, http://www.singletracks.com/south-carolina-bike-trails_39.html.

WHERE TO RIDE

Mountain biking isn't confined to the mountains of the Carolinas. Even if you live at the coast, odds are there's a trail network near you. The following list of thirty top rides in the Southeast includes four rides at the coast, ten in the high country, and sixteen in the Piedmont/Midlands, showing you don't need a mountain to mountain bike.

Mountain biking sites in the Carolinas

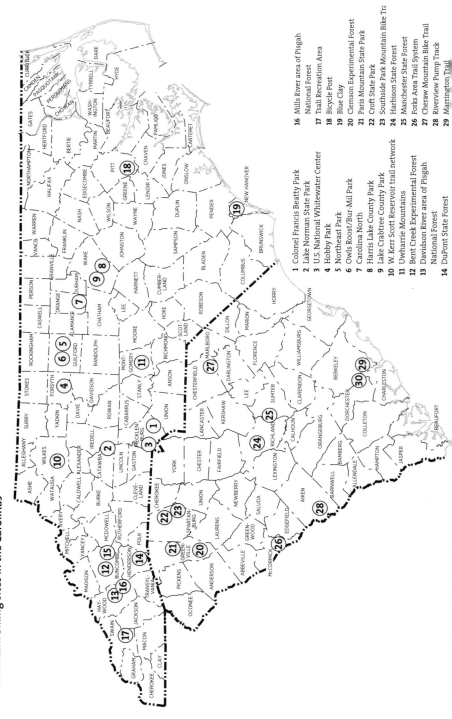

1 Colonel Francis Beatty Park
2 Lake Norman State Park
3 U.S. National Whitewater Center
4 Hobby Park
5 Northeast Park
6 Owls Roost/Bur-Mil Park
7 Carolina North
8 Harris Lake County Park
9 Lake Crabtree County Park
10 W. Kerr Scott Reservoir trail network
11 Uwharrie Mountains
12 Bent Creek Experimental Forest
13 Davidson River area of Pisgah National Forest
14 DuPont State Forest
16 Mills River area of Pisgah National Forest
17 Tsali Recreation Area
18 Bicycle Post
19 Blue Clay
20 Clemson Experimental Forest
21 Paris Mountain State Park
22 Croft State Park
23 Southside Park Mountain Bike Tra
24 Harbison State Forest
25 Manchester State Forest
26 Forks Area Trail System
27 Cheraw Mountain Bike Trail
28 Riverview Pump Track
29 Marrington Trail

North Carolina

Charlotte

1. Colonel Francis Beatty Park, 4330 Weddington Road. 5.75 miles.
Relatively flat single-track loop that's mildly technical. Good beginner
venue. More info: 704-643-5725; Tarheel TrailBlazers, http://www.tar
heeltrailblazers.com/TrailsReview1.cfm?trailid=6

2. Lake Norman State Park, 159 Inland Sea Lane, Troutman. 17.5 miles.
Rare North Carolina state park single-track known for good flow and
opportunities for beginners and advanced riders alike. More info:
704-528-6350; Tarheel TrailBlazers, http://www.tarheeltrailblazers
.com/TrailsReview1.cfm?trailid=60

3. U.S. National Whitewater Center, 5000 Whitewater Center Parkway. 17 miles. Well-groomed, well-marked trail network with good
mix of beginner, intermediate, and advanced trail. Bike rental included with price of admission, though you only need to pay parking
fee to ride the trails. More info: 704-391-3900; usnwc.org

Other trails of note: North Meck, Huntersville; Beech Springs/Poplar
Tent, Concord; Sherman Branch, Midland; Anne Close Springs Greenway, Fort Mill, S.C.

Triad

4. Hobby Park, 2301 West Clemmonsville Road, Winston-Salem.
7 miles. Long-standing Triad mountain biking tradition. Geared
toward more advanced riders. More info: 336-727-8000; Singletracks
.com, www.singletracks.com/bike-trails/hobby-park.html

5. Northeast Park, 3421 Northeast Park Dr., Gibsonville (use
4010 High Rock Road for GPS purposes). 5 miles. New network
that is gaining a reputation for fast flow. More info: 336-375-2322;
www.northeastpark.info/

6. Owls Roost/Bur-Mil Park, 5834 Bur-Mil Club Road, Greensboro.
5 miles. An oldie and enduring goldie for good reason: one, the flow

has been compared to a good mountain ride, and two, the trail connects with others in Greensboro's vast Watershed Lakes trail network. More info: 336-373-3800; http://burmil.guilfordparks.com/

Other trails of note: Country Park, Bald Eagle, Wild Turkey, Reedy Fork, Lake Brandt, and Hagen Stone, all in Greensboro; Salem Lake, Horizon Park, and Tanglewood in Winston-Salem.

Triangle

7. Carolina North, 1089 Municipal Drive, Chapel Hill. 20 miles (approximate). Mileage includes official trail on 750-acre holding of the University of North Carolina at Chapel Hill and adjoining unofficial trail behind Seawell Elementary School. Mix of double and single track. More info: 919-883-8930; TriangleMTB, http://www.trianglemtb.com/chapelhill.php

8. Harris Lake County Park, 2112 County Park Dr., New Hill. 8 miles. Clearly marked beginner, intermediate, and advanced trails, though advanced trail includes ride-arounds, making even the toughest trail accessible to most riders. More info: 919-387-4342; TriangleMTB, www.trianglemtb.com/harris.php

9. Lake Crabtree County Park, 1400 Aviation Parkway, Morrisville. 8 miles. The most popular trail network in the Triangle, in part because of its central location, in part because it's very beginner friendly. Adjoins more challenging bandit trail and thirteen miles of bike and bridle trail at neighboring Umstead State Park. More info: 919-460-3390; TriangleMTB, www.trianglemtb.com/crabtree.php

Other trails of note: Little River Regional Park, Durham; Briar Chapel, Chapel Hill; New Light and Beaverdam, Falls Lake State Recreation Area, Wake Forest; Legend Park, Clayton; Garner Recreation Park, Garner.

Elsewhere in the Piedmont

10. W. Kerr Scott Reservoir trail network, Wilkesboro. 35 miles. Dark Mountain, Overmountain Victory Trail, Fish Dam Creek Trail, and Warrior Creek trails are popular biking destinations. Get in shape, then

Dark Mountain near Wilkesboro is a popular trail network, especially for races such as the Burn 24 Hour Challenge.

come ride for the weekend on these well-designed and maintained trails. Beginners should start with the Overmountain Victory Trail. More info: Brushy Mountain Cyclists Club, http://www.bmcc.us/kerr_scott.htm

11. Uwharrie Mountains, 10 miles west of Troy on NC 24/27. 22 miles. Longtime trail network underwent a facelift in 2011, to rave reviews. Wood Run is 11 miles of easy, aerobic fire road; Supertree is 5 miles of easy-to-moderate single track; Keyauwee is 6 miles of more challenging single track. More info: http://www.uwharries.com/what-to-do/item/37-bike-the-uwharries.html; Tarheel TrailBlazers, http://www.tarheeltrailblazers.com/TrailsReview1.cfm?trailid=52

MOUNTAINS

12. Bent Creek Experimental Forest, Asheville. 24 miles. A big trail network of single track and double track on its own that connects with other trails in the region to create some truly epic rides. Proximity to Asheville makes it especially popular. More info: 828-667-5261; http://www.mtbikewnc.com/trailheads/pisgah-national-forest/pisgah-ranger-district/bent-creek/

13. Davidson River area of Pisgah National Forest, Brevard. 100+ miles. Davidson River campground makes a great base camp for exploring this vast network of trail; the Pisgah Center for Wildlife Education and Fish Hatchery is where several of the top trails depart. Some trails are only open to mountain biking from mid-October into spring. More info: MTB WNC, http://www.mtbikewnc.com/trail-heads/pisgah-national-forest/pisgah-ranger-district/davidson-river/

14. DuPont State Forest, between Hendersonville and Brevard. About 100 miles of all kinds of trail, from challenging double track to challenging single track to slickrock. Great scenery, with lots of waterfalls. More info: http://www.dupontforest.com/about.html

15. Kitsuma, Old Fort. 10 miles. The climb up 14 switchbacks is a grind, but the payoff is four miles of fast, rolling, mostly downhill that make Kitsuma a Pisgah classic. More info: Singletracks.com, http://www.singletracks.com/bike-trails/kitsuma.html

16. Mills River area of Pisgah National Forest, Mills River. 82 miles. Adjoining the Davidson River area, this is another classic Pisgah collection. Most notable are the Fletcher Creek and Laurel Mountain trails. More info: MTB WNC, http://www.mtbikewnc.com/trailheads/pisgah-national-forest/pisgah-ranger-district/mills-river/

17. Tsali Recreation Area, NC 28 at FS 1286, Bryson City area. 40 miles. Fee. Long noted for its great flow and mileage, Tsali consists of four big loops. Mountain bikers, hikers, and equestrians share the trails, with usage determined by day of the week. More info: MTB WNC, http://www.mtbikewnc.com/trailheads/nantahala-national-forest/cheoah-ranger-district/tsali-recreation-area/

COAST

18. Bicycle Post, Short Bridge Road near Kings Crossing Road, Greenville. 10 miles. $2 fee for non EC Velo Club members. Lots of trail on a small parcel of private land (hence the fee) and a remarkable—this is the Coastal Plain, after all—500 feet of vertical climbing throughout. More info: 252-756-3301; http://bicyclepost.com

19. Blue Clay, 3950 Juvenile Center Road, Castle Hayne (Wilmington area). 7 miles. Good example of a great bandit trail network evolving into a great legal network. More technical challenge than you might expect at the coast. More info: Singletracks.com, http://www.singletracks.com/bike-trails/blue-clay-road-trails.html

Other trails of note: Stoney Creek Trail, Jacksonville; Brunswick Nature Park, Wilmington area.

South Carolina

UPCOUNTRY

Greenville

20. Clemson Experimental Forest, Lake Hartwell. 87 miles total. This trail network exists primarily to service the 17,000-acre research forest. Thus, much of the trail system may not be what comes to mind when mountain bikers think of riding. Recommended trails include the 7.8-mile Issaqueena Lake Trail, Fants Grove (4.3 miles), and Quarry (5.9 miles). More info: http://www.clemson.edu/cafls/cef/

21. Paris Mountain State Park, 2401 State Park Road, Greenville. 15 miles. Closed to mountain biking on Saturdays. Trails are geared more toward intermediate and more experienced riders. More info: Singletracks.com, http://www.singletracks.com/bike-trails/paris-mountain-state-park.html

Spartanburg

22. Croft State Park, 450 Croft State Park Road. 20 miles. Good flow—and one of the more challenging trail networks in the state. Intermediate and up. More info: 864-585-1283; Singletracks.com, http://www.singletracks.com/bike-trails/croft-passage.html

23. Southside Park Mountain Bike Trail, 201 Gibson Rd. 8 miles. Good flow, good scenery. More info: Singletracks.com, http://www.singletracks.com/bike-trails/southside-park.html

Other trails of note: Tour de Dump, Spartanburg; Sadlers Creek State Recreation Area, Anderson County; Timmons Park, Greenville County; Palmetto Trail (statewide).

MIDLANDS

Columbia

24. Harbison State Forest, Lost Creek Drive and Broad River Road, Columbia area. 20 miles. Fee. A good mix of beginner, intermediate, and advanced trails make this network a go-to for Columbians looking for an after-work ride. More info: 803-896-8890; South Carolina Forestry Commission, http://www.state.sc.us/forest/refhartg.htm

25. Manchester State Forest, 6740 Headquarters Road, Wedgefield. 17.6 miles. You'll find lots of easy riding on long, sandy trails and some surprising challenge. Main trails: Killer 3 (10 miles), Hardcore (2.5), and Campbell Pond (2.6). More info: 803-494-8196; South Carolina State Trails Program, http://www.sctrails.net/Trails/alltrails/mountainbike/ManchesterForest.html

26. Forks Area Trail System, Sumter National Forest, NC 28 at Deepstep Road, Clarks Hill. 37 miles. Six loops, 37 miles of total riding, and few technical challenges make FATS, as it's acronymically known, a popular weekend destination for beginners. More info: SORBA CSRA, http://www.sorbacsra.org/Trails/FATS.htm

27. Cheraw Mountain Bike Trail, 100 State Park Road, Cheraw. 9.2 miles. Fast trail through a pine and hardwood forest on a sandy

—but not too sandy—surface. More info: 843-5379656, South Carolina State Trails Program, http://www.sctrails.net/Trails/alltrails/mountainbike/CherawMtBike.html

28. Riverview Pump Track, 100 Riverview Park Dr., North Augusta. Pump track. More info: 803-441-4311; Singletracks.com, www.singletracks.com/bike-trails/riverview-pump-track.html

Other trails of note: Baker Creek State Park, Stevens Creek/Turkey Creek, Hickory Knob State Resort Park, McCormick County; Horn Creek, Edgefield County; Sesquicentennial State Park, Richland County; Palmetto Trail (statewide).

LOW COUNTRY

Charleston

29. Marrington Trail, Goose Creek (part of Marrington Plantation/Joint Base Charleston). 12 miles. Mix of flat, flowy, nontechnical single track with a pump track worked in for younger riders. More info: Singletracks.com, http://www.singletracks.com/bike-trails/marrington-trail.html

30. Wannamaker North Trail, Wannamaker County Park, 8888 University Boulevard, North Charleston. 8 miles. Fee. Fast, smooth trail in 1,015-acre park. More info: 843-572-7275; Singletracks.com, http://www.singletracks.com/bike-trails/wannamaker-park.html

Other trails of note: Boyd Pond, Beech Island; Horry County Bike Run Park, Myrtle Beach.

Flat-Water Paddling

Sounds, swamps, blackwater rivers, lakes, oh my!

WHAT IT'S ABOUT

The channel of tidal Upper Rantowles Creek narrowed, the two-foot-tall cordgrass closing in from both sides until the creek was maybe ten feet wide. We could still see pines and live oak laden with Spanish moss on more solid ground inland. But on this particular stretch it was the sky that dominated.

"The clouds are really wonderful," Christina, the naturalist on our trip, commented. The sky directly above was a nonthreatening mix of wispy altocumulus and cirrus clouds. To the east over the Atlantic some billowy cumulus clouds had gathered, though they too appeared nonthreatening and seemed to be moving out to sea anyway. It was a typical mid-December sky, a winter sky that appeared indecisive and indifferent. For several minutes we sat and watched as it went about its slow dance. The sky was a gift, especially since the day had begun with predawn thunder, lightening, and rain, and the forecast for the day had called for more of the same.

Shortly, the creek began to widen and our environs, a marsh reclaimed from a long-abandoned rice field dating back to the late 1700s, reclaimed our attention. We put our paddles on autopilot and made slow progress against a tide a half hour from turning in our favor. It was about this time that something I'd learned back at the put-in made me realize just how good the flat-water paddling in the Carolinas is. There were nine of us on the trip, seven of whom were avid—meaning they get out once a week—paddlers. Yet only three had previously paddled Upper Rantowles Creek. That this collection of paddling experience was relatively unfamiliar with this gem underscored the plethora of worthy options at our disposal.

Paddlers from the Carolina Sea Kayak Meetup group set out from
Bulow Landing for a paddle on Rantowles Creek in Charlotte.

"I live ten minutes from here," the semiretired Dennis told me, "and
I've never been here. Heck, I'm ten minutes from Folly Landing, fifteen
minutes from Sandy Point, and fifteen minutes from Kiawah."

Driving down from North Carolina I'd already taken note of the
options—from the vantage point of a Honda Civic on I-95, no less. I
crossed South Carolina's Black River, and even in the gray of a cloudy
dawn could see the potential of this swampy paddle. Ditto a few miles
down the interstate where the Pocotaligo River didn't so much flow
under the road at a given point, but sieved beneath on an extended
elevated stretch. Even massive Lake Marion, which at 110,000 acres
is South Carolina's largest lake, looked promising. Such size typically
suggests a lake made for power boats. Yet there were intimate nooks
here where paddlers could explore relatively wake-free.

The drive made me realize that there's a lot more diversity to flat-
water paddling than the phrase suggests.

Lakes

At 4:30 on a Friday afternoon there was a steady rain, the same steady
rain that had been falling for most of the past two days. At 4:40 the

rain stopped, and at 4:45 the gray sky began to lighten. At 4:46 I was putting the kayak on the car and heading west, to Jordan Lake. Within half an hour, I would be on the water.

The most accessible flat-water paddling for most Carolinians is a local lake. Between manmade lakes created for water supplies or flood control and the occasional naturally occurring lake, odds are there's at least one lake within a half hour of where you live. Within thirty minutes of my house in Cary, North Carolina, part of the Research Triangle, there are three major lakes (Falls and Jordan, both state recreation areas, and Harris) and thirteen flood control lakes. Most of those lakes have at least one boat access, and four have onsite boat rentals. It doesn't get much easier to get out and explore than that. Which is why paddling may be a more accessible option than you might think.

For much of the summer, I'd been threatening to end a workweek with a paddle in my hands. For a variety of not-really-good-enough reasons, it still hadn't happened. Since I couldn't come up with a not-good-enough reason to stay home, and because at one point I actually thought I'd seen the sun poke through, I found myself unloading my Old Town Loon 100 recreational kayak at the Ebenezer Church boat ramp at Jordan Lake.

Two things to like about this particular put-in from a kayaker's perspective: One, like so many boat launches, it's operated by the N.C. Wildlife Resources Commission and is a twenty-four-hour launch. Put in whenever; take out whenever. Stay on the water as long as you like, provided you've got the required lights. Watch the sun set? Might as well stay on the water and watch the stars come out.

Two, while the vast majority of motor boats head west from here, to the main body of Jordan Lake, the savvy kayaker heads east, under the Beaver Creek Road bridge to the relative peace and quiet of two Jordan fingers that eventually dissolve into Beaver and Little Beaver creeks, both ideal for winding down a long week in the trenches. This is common at many larger lakes in the Carolinas: while their vast main bodies may attract speedy, wake-making power boats, their spindly fingers create nooks and crannies ideal for exploring by small craft.

Their abundance makes lakes an attractive local option. But lakes can also be worth traveling for. This is especially true of mountain lakes, where experiences intimate and expansive can be had. The intimate are perhaps the most common, on small, cozy lakes, often dammed, often associated with some sort of resort. Some are attached to campground resorts, some to exclusive summer getaways.

Your luck may be better on a larger lake. North Carolina's Lake Lure, dubbed by *National Geographic* as one of the "ten most spectacular man-made lakes in the world," is 720 acres of water in the Hickory Nut Gorge region. And South Carolina's Lake Jocassee, at 7,500 acres, is popular among paddlers for its various fingers poking into the Blue Ridge Escarpment. Waterfalls are common sites where feeder creeks abruptly tumble into the lake.

Sounds

The November light was fading fast and between the graying sky and the maze of cordgrass I couldn't tell how much progress I'd made, how much farther I had to go. The steady slurp of the brackish water slapping the kayak's stern suggested I was making progress. But how much? My biggest concern was that the light would fade to the point I could no longer see the bobbing paddle-trail markers ahead. A couple years earlier I'd proven myself capable of losing the bright white marker atop an orange post on a sunny day. What if I couldn't find the markers now, in the approaching gloaming?

Shortly, the tight channel I'd been in widened and I could see a marker fifty yards ahead, on the right. Then another, and finally another before the bluff on the east end of Bear Island came into view. A good sight, for just beyond the bluff was the inlet I sought, the inlet where I could beach for the evening and set up camp. The twinge of concern vanished, the joy of the paddle returned. Nothing like a jolt of uncertainty to spice up a trip.

That's part of the joy of paddling the Carolinas' more intimate sounds, that water between mainland and barrier island protected from the powerful Atlantic but rife with untamed adventure. Well, except in the case of Bear Island, where the 2.6-mile canoe trail is well blazed, taking at least some of the mystery out of paddling a tidal marsh maze.

Paddling in the tidal marsh of a sound isn't tricky for the beginner, but there are some things you need to be aware of:

The tide. Check the tide and paddle with it. If you're heading from the mainland to a barrier island, as is the case with the Hammocks Beach/Bear Island trip, paddle out as the tide is going out, paddle back when the tide is coming in. Local tide tables are easy to find along the coast, either online or in a local visitors guide.

The weather. Check the forecast before heading out, and keep a constant watch on the sky. Summer thunderstorms in particular can build fast along the coast; the last place you want to be when you start hearing thunder is on open water.

Wayfinding. Even with a good map a tidal marsh can be tricky to navigate. What may look at first like a solid channel can close up around the next bend. This adds to the experience—to a point. To avoid adding more to the experience than you'd like, check for local marked paddle trails or look into clubs and outfitters that lead guided trips. I might still be on Upper Rantowles Creek had not a fellow paddler shown up with a GPS bearing a track he'd made on a previous outing. Outfitters, of course, will charge for their services; clubs will not, but you'll need all of your own equipment.

Swamps

If ever there is the potential to get lost on water, it's in a swamp. Part of what makes a swamp paddle a swamp paddle are the mix of obstacles —the stentorian cypress and tupelo gum, the clusters of assorted bays, the live oaks festooned with Spanish moss—that pepper the still waters. Picture 760 acres of this and you've got Merchants Millpond in the northeast corner of North Carolina.

Now, 760 acres of this may not seem like much—until you've been slowly paddling in it for a couple hours, then realize it's time to head back and—

Where the heck are we?

That's where Deborah and Lisa, two paddlers from Durham, found themselves one Sunday evening in the summer of 2011. "We turned to head back, and had no idea where we were," recalls Lisa.

They readily acknowledged their bafflement, but continued paddling in the direction they thought they had come from. They looked for familiar sights, but it all looked the same. They looked for the sun,

Duckweed covers the surface at Merchants Millpond. The state park rents canoes and has a marked trail to guide you through the swamp.

having vaguely thought they'd paddled out west to east, but it was a milky late-afternoon fall sky and there was little hint of where the sun was—or was heading. They thought to check a compass, then realized they didn't have one. So on they paddled.

An hour passed, then another thirty minutes. Their pace picked up but it was almost like they were on a treadmill: the same scenery —great scenery, but always the same—kept rolling by. Soon, the light got "to that point." "I got out my phone and called the park office, 'We're lost.'"

"What do you see around you?" asked the ranger. He listened to Lisa's brief description, then said, "We'll be there in about five minutes."

Not always the case in a swamp. Even when there's a marked paddle trail, as there is at Merchants Millpond, it's easy to get sidetracked. When paddling a swamp, always take a compass and brush up on your orienteering skills. If your navigational skills aren't so good, find a guided trip. There are lots of them.

Rivers

Flat-water river options abound in the Carolinas. They require more planning, primarily in the form of setting a shuttle. And they require more attention to detail in general. A little story from my early days, about a river trip where everything that could go wrong—leaving the keys for the shuttle car in the car at the put-in; forgetting the first-aid kit, throw line, and guidebook; leaving the boat in the river—did.

It was a Sunday in March and our plan was to do an eight-mile stretch of the Cape Fear River between Lillington and Erwin. Originally, six boats were scheduled to do the trip. Then five. Then, at the last minute, three. That, I later learned from my paddling mentor, Joe Jacob, was the bare minimum we should have had on unfamiliar water.

"Ideally," Joe told me later, "it's best to have at least three boats on a trip." Your better paddlers can go first to identify a good route through rapids and run sweep in case anything happens to the middle boat. Also, if one boat gets into a jam, one boat can go for help while the other stays with the one in trouble.

Another problem arose when two inexperienced paddlers showed up for the trip. I had selected a stretch of the Cape Fear with a couple of Class II rapids based on the experience level of the original group. Rah and Iva had some paddling experience, but they had never paddled together, and they were in a rented boat.

Joe chuckled at the first dilemma. "When I take a group out, I do a little exercise before we get in the water. I'll stand in the boat—on land—and get someone to stand in the boat with me. 'Everything about our relationship just got in the boat with us,' I tell them." That, he said, leads to a discussion about communication and the roles each paddler plays and the importance of talking to one another.

Yet another problem: their rental was a tandem kayak, an Old Town Loon 138T.

"I wouldn't put a double kayak on that stretch of river," Joe said. He noted that most outfitters wouldn't let such a boat go out the door if they knew it was destined for the Cape Fear. That led to talk about the importance of checking up on a river before heading out, especially if you're trying a new section. Ask someone who's paddled the river. Ask an outfitter ("We get thirty to thirty-five calls a day from people wanting information about local rivers," Joe said). Consult a guidebook.

The first four miles, on flat water, went well, a brisk current helping us along. Then we started to hit some ledges, one-foot drops that we negotiated pretty easily. Soon, the mild roar up ahead suggested something more challenging, so we pulled over to scout. Finally, a smart move.

There was an island, to the left of which was a relatively passive stretch of water. To the right were three channels, including a severe dogleg with a gradual drop to the right and a tree-obscured passage to the left. Down the middle was a quick chute bordered by a boulder on the right and followed up by a nasty strainer to the left. We decided on the center chute of the right-hand passage.

James, in a twelve-foot recreational kayak, went first. Later, he told us that he felt the current push him toward the boulder, but paddling in a small, responsive boat, he was able to quickly correct and zip through. Rah and Iva weren't so lucky.

They, too, felt the current, but in their larger boat and without the benefit of having paddled together, they were dashed against the rock and promptly capsized.

Joe revisited the communication theme. "It's possible that on their approach they didn't understand their roles." In a canoe, it's a little more clear-cut: the paddler in the bow generally scouts and provides momentum, the paddler in the stern steers. Those roles are a little fuzzier in a kayak.

Joe was impressed by Rah and Iva's recovery. They quickly emptied the boat, then pulled the kayak over the boulder and put it back in in a relatively calm pool on the downstream side.

A quarter mile downstream we hit another ledge. James went first, I followed. We pulled into an eddy and chatted. When Rah and

Iva didn't appear within a reasonable amount of time we glanced up river to discover that—*huh!*—their boat had gone over the ledge backward. Worse, on the descent its stern managed to wedge between submerged rocks. Half the boat was under water, the other half jutted out at a 45-degree angle.

"It looks like the *Titanic*," James said.

Indeed it did, though in this case the boat would go down no more. Nor would it come out. The weight of the water coupled with the wedge factor made the blue Loon one immovable object.

James and I beached our boats and ran back up the bank. "They were a good thirty yards out," I explained to Joe, "and even if I'd had a throw line"—and at this Joe's eyebrows raised, effectively cutting me off. With a throw line, Joe explained, we would have had several options. If the boat truly were anchored, we could have tossed them the line, had them tie it off to the boat, then used it as a ferry line for them to make their way hand-over-hand to shore. Or, we could have simply tossed them the rope, had them grab on, and let the pendulum effect swing them back to shore just downstream.

As it was, their only option was to abandon ship and swim, never a good option in cold water in a strong current.

From there, things went pretty much according to standard emergency plan. James and I packed extra clothes, which Rah and Iva immediately changed into. They drank plenty of liquids to rehydrate themselves, and they downed a fair amount of gorp to replenish their energy levels. Then, it was time for a long march through the woods to civilization.

"Still," I told Joe, "it felt pretty helpless to stand on the shore and not be able to help."

"I was on the Nantahala one day about twenty years ago," Joe said, "and this guy came over Little Falls and got tossed out of his boat. He got caught in a hydraulic [swirling water], and I thought he was dead. Finally, he pops up, only to get hit in the head by a canoe. Then I really thought he was dead. He popped up yet again and got hit by a raft. The fourth time he had the presence of mind to hold his hand above his head, and he managed to grab the rope on another raft that passed over him.

"I walked right over to the [Nantahala Outdoor Center] and signed up for a water-rescue class," Joe said. "I never wanted to feel that help-less again."

Moral: a little preparation, a little forethought, can go a long way on a river trip.

Or any trip, for that matter.

DETAILS, DETAILS

What you need to know to get started flat-water paddling.

Where do people paddle flat water in the Carolinas? Statewide, even in the mountains. Let's start there, where you'll find one of the largest bodies of water in the Carolinas, Lake Jocassee. The manmade lake's 7,500 acres include gorgelike coves that are popular with kayakers. Dammed bodies of water abound in the mountains and are popular with kayakers and canoeists alike. Moving into the Piedmont and the Midlands, the Carolina's population centers are graced with good pad-dling options, often within just a few minutes' drive. The Triangle area of North Carolina, for instance, has three major lakes—Falls, Harris, and Jordan—and numerous smaller lakes, many of which offer rent-als in warmer weather. This region also boasts numerous mellow rivers with mellow currents. For example, the Congaree River, which brings the blackwater experience of the coast to residents of Colum-bia. But it is the coast that's so often associated with the Carolina's quintessential flat-water paddling experience. The sprawling Coastal Plain as it nears the Atlantic has seemingly endless swamp and back-water paddling options. The North Carolina Paddle Trails Association has documented more than 2,500 miles of paddle trail in North Caro-lina alone. And at the coast itself, there's the experience of exploring marshes and sounds and the backsides of barrier islands, and the thrill of ocean kayaking as well. In the Carolinas, you're never far from flat-water paddling.

How to get started. There are several ways for the novice to dip his or her paddle. If the weather is warm, odds are there's a lake near you that rents canoes and/or kayaks, usually for a nominal fee ($5 an hour or less). Pick a warm afternoon and introduce yourself. If you're more comfortable having someone show you the basics and be there to answer questions, many parks—state and local—offer guided trips. They're usually an hour or so, with all the equipment provided, and they're usually free. Once you get a little more comfortable on the water and want to venture beyond the neighborhood lake, join a paddling club. These clubs have long existed but have proliferated in the Meetup.com age. I've listed some clubs below; to find paddlers near you, go to Meetup.com, click "Find a Meetup Group," and search for "paddling" within however far a range you're willing to travel from your zip code. Meetups are typically led by a core group of enthusiasts who organize trips within your region. They're often people who have been at it for a while, are passionate, and are eager to share that passion. Flat-water paddling is one of the easiest adventure pursuits to get started in.

Cost. Your first couple of times, you'll likely rent a boat. At a local lake, you'll pay around $5 for an hour's time on the water. Rates pick up when you have to transport a boat and use it for a day; in this case, expect to pay $35 to $50 for a quality boat. Soon, though, you'll be done with renting; it's time to buy. The price of a kayak or canoe can vary wildly. Interested in a simple little recreational kayak for exploring smaller bodies of water? You can score a sturdy boat for around $300. Once you start getting into performance issues, the price of a boat rises. If you want a boat you can paddle for longer distances, that will track well and cut through the water, you're looking to spend a minimum of $600–$700. And if you get into touring and crave a light, fast boat with plenty of secure storage, you're looking at a fiberglass boat that can run you $4,000 or more. It's the same with paddles: you can spend $50 for a basic paddle that's made of stout (read: heavy) material, or you can spend $500 for a lightweight carbon paddle ergonomically designed to minimize the strain of a long day on the water. A personal flotation device (PFD) ($50 and up), drybag to store your valuables ($10), and car rack to tote your boat ($150 and up) are some of the other basics you'll need. Once you're outfitted, gas will be your main expense.

Related associations and organizations. To find paddle trails and destinations throughout North Carolina, visit the North Carolina Paddle Trails Association at ncpaddletrails.info. Sea Kayak Carolina in the

Charleston area has an extensive rundown of destinations and paddling resources (tide and current weather conditions) on its Web site, seakayakcarolina.com. There are various canoe and kayak clubs operating throughout the Carolinas. Clubs are a great way to hook up with more experienced paddlers who can share insights on gear, technique, and places to paddle. Some of those clubs: Carolina Kayak Club in the Triangle area, carolinakayakclub.org; Carolina Canoe Club, throughout the Carolinas, carolinacanoeclub.org; Lowcountry Paddlers in the Charleston area, lowcountrypaddlers.net; Palmetto Paddlers in the Columbia area, palmettopaddlers.org. You'll find more paddle clubs through Meetup.com. Search "paddling" within the distance of your zip code that you're comfortable traveling and you'll likely come up with more than one option.

Commitment. Of all the pursuits in this book, this one probably relies the least on practice to retain competence. Learning proper paddle strokes will make the experience less tiring and more enjoyable, but the technique is fairly simple and straightforward, not something you need extensive practice to perfect. It will behoove you, however, to maintain a modicum of upper body and core strength. Check out recommended exercises at paddling.net.

Physical and mental demands. The biggest physical demand may simply be staying seated for extended periods on long trips (two hours or longer). Modern kayaks have more sophisticated seat systems that allow you to adjust seat angle and positioning, reducing the likelihood of strain from staying put for too long. And, as mentioned above, it's a good idea to maintain a decent level of upper body and core strength. Mentally, well, that's one of the key reasons people paddle flat water. This is one sport that allows your mind to drift, that lets your motor—your body—go into autopilot as you take in your surroundings. Which isn't to say you can blank completely. In some swamp or marsh settings you may need to follow trail markers to keep from getting lost (Merchants Millpond and the paddle trail from Hammocks Beach to Bear Island both come to mind; I've become . . . disoriented at both places). It's also imperative that you keep an eye on the weather (open water isn't a fun place to be in a storm) and be keyed into tides and current in coastal environments. By and large, though, your brain gets a rest on flat water.

Is it seasonal? No. If you don't like cold weather, then you probably won't like being on the water when the temperature drops. But if you're dressed for cold weather—and yes, there are plenty of opportunities to spend money on cold-weather paddle gear—late fall into early spring can be the best time of year to paddle, the absence of greenery opening the landscape for better wildlife viewing.

Competitive element. You'll find flat-water races, but speed is not the reason the majority of people paddle. Rather, it's the opportunity to escape a fast-paced world.

Folks who do this also tend to . . . do other contemplative activities, such as hiking.

Are the Carolinas a mecca for this activity? It's hard to imagine better flat-water paddling options than those abundant in the coastal Carolinas. An abundance of barrier islands create a variety of open-water options on sounds and more intimate paddling through marshes; blackwater rivers and swamps result in mesmerizing inland trips, paddling amid cypress and tupelo dating back nearly 2,000 years. The resource has long been there, but only since the 1990s, with the growing promotion of the region's paddle trails, has the extent of paddling options available become widely known.

Hot spots elsewhere. You needn't go far to find more great flat-water paddling. Georgia and Florida both have excellent flat-water paddling in abundance. Ditto the coast of Maine and the Puget Sound area of Washington State.

Resources. See "Related associations and organizations" above. *Paddling Eastern North Carolina*, 2nd ed., by Paul Ferguson (Raleigh: Pocosin Press, 2007), http://www.pocosinpress.com/; *Paddling South Carolina: A Guide to Palmetto State River Trails*, rev. ed., by Gene Able and Jack Horan (Orangeburg, S.C.: Sandlapper Publishing Company, 2001).

Flat-water paddling sites in the Carolinas

1 Bear Island
2 Merchants Millpond
3 Black River
4 Roanoke River
5 Price Lake
6 Mountain Island Lake
7 Catawba River
8 Lake Brandt
9 High Point Lake/
  City Lake Park

11 Neuse River
12 Beaverdam area of Falls
   Lake State Recreation Area
13 Haw River
14 Zeke's Island
15 Folly Island
16 Goodale State Park millpond
17 Edisto River
18 Lake Jocassee
19 Rantowles Creek

WHERE TO PADDLE FLAT WATER

You'll find flat water throughout the Carolinas, from high-mountain lakes to Piedmont rivers to the tidal marshes and sounds of the coast. The states' geographic diversity results in a variety of flat-water paddling options—and lots of them. The recommendations below aren't intended as a "best of" list for each type of paddling. Rather, they're popular representations of what you'll find that for various reasons —ease of access, nearby rentals—are especially good options for beginners.

Definitions: sound paddles are those between the mainland and barrier islands; swamp paddles are through typical cypress and tupelo gum wetlands of the coast; blackwater is moving tannic water that, despite its dark appearance, can be some of the cleanest water around; mountain lakes are high-country impoundments suitable for paddling; and close to home is a collection of popular paddles close to the population centers of the Carolinas.

North Carolina

SOUND

1. Bear Island, Hammocks Beach State Park, Swansboro. Perhaps the most accessible barrier-island paddle along the coast, thanks to a marked 2.6-mile canoe trail that leads you through the marsh to the island's east end. Pull up in a protected inlet and explore; better yet, bring your camping gear and take advantage of one of a dozen primitive camp sites on the island. Best time to visit: November through March, when the passenger ferry isn't running, leaving the island exclusively to paddlers such as yourself. More info: North Carolina State Parks, http://www.ncparks.gov/Visit/parks/habe/main.php

SWAMP

2. Merchants Millpond, Merchants Millpond State Park, Gatesville. Perhaps the most accessible swamp paddle in the Carolinas. This 760-acre one-time millpond is now, 190 years later, a paddle-friendly swamp where you can rent a canoe year-round and paddle beneath bald cypress and tupelo gum trees and atop floating green and red mats of pea-size duckweed and yellow cow lily, while listening to every frog known to eastern North Carolina: carpenter frogs, leopard frogs, bull frogs, cricket frogs, and assorted tree frogs. Great beginner paddle. More info: North Carolina State Parks, http://www.ncparks.gov/Visit/parks/memi/ecology.php

SLACKWATER

3. Black River, Ivanhoe. The Black River drains portions of Sampson, Bladen, and Pender counties in the southeast Coastal Plain before giving it up to the Cape Fear River above Wilmington. Along the way, the river is renowned for its water quality, among the best in the Southeast. And in sections, including the 7.6 miles below Ivanhoe, it is known for its remarkable blackwater scenery, weaving in and out of some of the oldest cypress trees in the country, at least one of which predates Christ. The girth of these behemoths gives the Black an otherworldly feel. More info: *Paddling Eastern North Carolina*, by Paul Ferguson; Great Outdoor Provision Co., http://greatoutdoorprovision.com/expert/black-river-section-5/

4. Roanoke River. The Roanoke meanders through the largest intact bottomland hardwood swamp east of the Mississippi. It drains an area of 9,680 square miles, is dense with vegetation, from the giant cypress on down, and has more than 200 bird species as well as black bear, river otter, deer, bobcats, beaver, and mink. Boy, that's a lot to see in just one day, you're probably thinking. Which is what the Roanoke River Partners thought when they decided to build a series of camping platforms from Weldon down to the Albemarle Sound. Sixteen had been completed by the end of 2012. More info: Roanoke River Partners, http://www.roanokeriverpartners.org/

MOUNTAIN LAKES

5. Price Lake, MP 297 of the Blue Ridge Parkway, Blowing Rock. Possibly the most accessible of the mountain lakes, Price Lake is part of the Julian Price Memorial Park located just down the road from Blowing Rock. The lake is just feet away from the parkway. It's rimmed with rhododendron and mountain laurel, and on a clear day there's a great view of Grandfather Mountain. During the warm-weather months there are canoe rentals. Classic Blue Ridge Parkway scenery with classic Blue Ridge Parkway convenience. More info: National Park Service, www.nps.gov/blri/

CLOSE TO HOME

Charlotte

6. Mountain Island Lake, Latta Plantation, Charlotte. If you need evidence of how popular Mountain Island Lake is as a Charlotte paddling destination, consider that it has its own dedicated kayaking club and sponsors an array of kayaking events, including sunset kayaking, yoga kayaking, kayak geocaching, and kayaking for homeschoolers. There are five access points to the lake, which has 61 miles of shoreline and 3,281 surface acres; perhaps the most paddle-friendly is at Latta Plantation Nature Center and Preserve, part of the Mecklenburg County Park and Recreation Department. More info: Mecklenburg County Park and Recreation, http://charmeck.org/mecklenburg/county/ParkandRec/StewardshipServices/NaturePreserves/Pages/Latta.aspx

7. Catawba River at the U.S. National Whitewater Center. The Catawba runs for 200 miles after departing the Asheville area and in spots is pretty frisky. But by the time it arrives in Charlotte it's fairly wide, easy flowing, and beginner friendly. A good spot for a beginner is around the National Whitewater Center, where, with the price of admission, you can try different boats—from solo sit-on-top kayaks to multiperson war canoes. More info: Great Outdoor Provision Co., http://greatoutdoorprovision.com/expert/catawba-river-national-whitewater-center/

Triad

8. Lake Brandt, Greensboro. Greensboro bumps its head against a roof of paddling in the three watershed lakes rimming the city on the north: Townsend, the biggest; Higgins, the smallest; and Brandt, which appears to be just right for paddling. Throaty power boats are attracted to Townsend; at 226 acres Higgins is a good destination, trumped by Brandt's 816 acres and multiple fingers for exploring. Rentals (canoes and kayaks) are available at both Brandt and Higgins. More info: Greensboro Parks and Recreation, http://www.greensboro-nc.gov/index.aspx?page=1317

9. High Point Lake/City Lake Park, High Point. Most Piedmont lakes are distinguished by craggy shorelines resulting from water seeping into every available finger. This is especially true at High Point Lake, its thin trunk and scalloped edges giving it something of a seahorse profile. This paddle is further enhanced by the fact the lake is part of the 376-acre Piedmont Environmental Center and is an especially popular spot for birding and wildlife watching of various sorts. More info: Great Outdoor Provision Co., http://greatoutdoorprovision.com/expert/high-point-lakecity-lake-park/

10. Dan River, Westfield. The Dan, which spills out of Virginia into North Carolina northwest of Hanging Rock, offers Triad paddlers a taste of mountain water. Much of that taste has a real zing, in the form of Class I-III whitewater. But there is a placid stretch that runs for 4.3 miles, from the Moore's Springs Campground Access to the Hanging Rock Access. OK, you may find a riffle or two, but this is largely flat-water fun, the type of friendly water outfitters like to put their novice paddlers on. More info: *Paddling Eastern North Carolina*, by Paul Ferguson; Great Outdoor Provision Co., http://greatoutdoorprovision.com/expert/dan-river/

Triangle

11. Neuse River, Raleigh. Nothing like having a year-round, reliable river running through town. That's the Neuse, which from the base of the Falls Lake Dam (which is responsible for that reliable river flow) runs 28 miles south through Raleigh into Johnston County. Right from the put-in just below the dam this is a surprisingly wild escape; in spots there may be less than 25 yards of riparian buffer between you and urban civilization, but the most you'll detect of the latter is the occasional *beep-beep-beep* of a dump truck backing up. And access is easy: in the city of Raleigh alone there are five put-ins along a

Paddling upstream on the dammed stretch of the Haw River above Saxapahaw.

17-mile stretch of the river. More info: *Paddling Eastern North Carolina*, by Paul Ferguson; City of Raleigh, http://www.raleighnc.gov/arts/content/PRecRecreation/Articles/AdventureCanoeSites.html

12. Beaverdam area of Falls Lake State Recreation Area, Wake Forest. Between Falls, Jordan, and Harris lakes, and dozens of smaller flood-control lakes, there's no shortage of paddling options in the Triangle. Beaverdam stands out because this isolated segment of Falls Lake is restricted to canoes, kayaks, and boats with trolling motors. Experience the open-water feel of a big lake by heading north from the put-in. Then, after a couple miles, paddle under Old Weaver Trail into a sprawling wetland fed by Robertson and Beaverdam creeks. More info: Great Outdoor Provision Co., http://greatoutdoorprovision.com/expert/falls-lake-beaverdam-recreation-area/

13. Haw River, above Saxapahaw. The Haw River west of Chapel Hill is a mix of rolling river, roiling whitewater, and stretches of dammed flat water. The latter offers a rarity in river paddling, the opportunity to put-in and take-out at the same spot. Probably the best spot for this in the region is on the more than 5 miles of dammed water from Saxapahaw upriver to Swepsonville. The put-in is easy, and if you're in need of a boat, Haw River Canoe and Kayak is right there. Après-paddle hang out in Saxapahaw, a revived mill town where you'll find cutting-edge cuisine, gourmet coffee, local brews on tap, and Ping-Pong for $2. More info: *Paddling Eastern North Carolina*, by Paul Ferguson; Great Outdoor Provision Co., http://greatoutdoorprovision.com/expert/haw-river-swepsonville-river-park-to-saxapahaw/

Wilmington

14. Zeke's Island, Kure Beach. The Zeke's Island National Estuarine Research Reserve is a 1,635-acre preserve offering the best in barrier island, beach, marsh, and tidal flats, all quickly accessible from a mainland put-in at Kure Beach. You'll find an impressive selection of shore birds here, thanks in part to the fact the estuary is a nursery to fish, shrimp, crabs, clams, and oysters. More info: North Carolina Coastal Reserve, http://www.nccoastalreserve.net/About-The-Reserve/Reserve-Sites/Zekes-Island/60.aspx

South Carolina

SOUND

15. Folly Island, Charleston. The Folly Beach area minutes from downtown Charleston is enormously popular, in part because it is minutes from downtown, but mainly because of the numerous tidal creeks behind the barrier island offer seemingly endless opportunities to explore a marsh environment. Dolphins and a wide variety of birds add to the area's allure. More info: Adventure Collective, http://advguides.com/charleston-adventures/charleston-paddling/1944/folly-river-to-bird-key-folly-beach/

16. Goodale State Park millpond, Camden. A Civil War–era millpond reverted to cypress swamp, this is one beginner-friendly swamp paddle. Onsite rentals and a marked, 3-mile paddle trail through the 140-acre lake further entrench Goodale as a great first-time swamp experience. More info: South Carolina State Parks, http://www.southcarolinaparks.com/goodale/introduction.aspx

BLACKWATER

17. Edisto River, South Carolina. The Edisto River Basin contains the longest free-flowing blackwater river in the country, working its way from the Midlands through 12 counties and into the Low Country. There are more than 50 river access points along the way, with options ranging from a nice day trip to a two-week river camping trip. Which part of the system you choose to paddle depends on where you are and how much time you have. More info: *Edisto River Companion*, by Ken C. Driggers (Columbia, S.C.: Palmetto Conservation Foundation/PCF Press, 2008); Friends of the Edisto, http://www.edistofriends.org/

MOUNTAIN LAKES

18. Lake Jocassee. You don't need to look long at a map of Lake Jocassee, on the North Carolina/South Carolina line (though mostly in South Carolina) to realize this giant lake has intimate paddling potential. While the bulk of the 7,500-acre lake is in three main channels feeding a central pool, dozens of small fingers exploring gorge-like nooks and crannies snaking into the surrounding mountains are perfect for paddling. Lots of waterfalls add to this mountain lake paddle. More info: www.paddling.net

CLOSE TO HOME

Charleston

19. Rantowles Creek. There are so many places for a paddler to explore in the Charleston area that deciding on one can be a chore.

Rantowles Creek gets the nod for one simple reason: I've paddled it. From the put-in at Bulow Landing go left and explore the various channels that weave in and out of the cordgrass and beneath live oaks tinseled with Spanish moss. The creek—and its numerous dead-end drainage feeders—explores a long-abandoned rice field. For a more efficient paddle time your trip with the tide. More info: www.seakayakcarolina.com

Columbia

20. Congaree River. In paddling circles, Columbia is best known for the Class II and III whitewater that courses through town courtesy of the Saluda River. But there's another, more tranquil experience to be enjoyed by Columbians on the Congaree River Blue Trail. The trail runs from Columbia to Congaree National Park. High bluffs and extensive floodplains mark the trip. More info: National Park Service, http://www.nps.gov/cong/planyourvisit/bluetrail.htm

Whitewater Paddling

Learn a valuable lesson from a don't-do-it-yourselfer.

WHAT IT'S ABOUT

Ron Wulff considers himself a very safety-conscious whitewater paddler. As a result, he offers this advice for folks interested in getting into the sport: don't do what I did.

"I met this guy through the Simply Kayaking Meetup," Ron says of his introduction to the sport, "and he said, 'Hey, you wanna paddle the Neuse?' and I said, 'Sure.'"

This occurred shortly after Ron had retired and gotten into paddling. He'd bought a 13.5-foot-long sit-on-top kayak on eBay and was looking for sit-on-top kind of fun. Which is to say, flat water, possibly with a mellow current, definitely with no rocks, and certainly no descending boulder fields creating boat-sucking hydraulics and monster waves to maneuver through. He was familiar with the Neuse, having paddled a stretch closer to his home outside Clayton, a stretch best known for its long, quiet passages along tree-lined banks. A stretch with one Class I rapid. A riffle, really.

The stretch of the Neuse he was about to paddle, though, was something of an anomaly.

"So we put in," Ron recalls, "and we do a couple of Class I rapids and I'm thinking, 'This is fun.' But then I notice the people up in front of us. They seemed to be going . . . *down*. Then I heard the noise."

Ron was approaching the one stretch on this otherwise placid 193-mile passage to the Atlantic with Class II water, the stretch through Raleigh right below where Crabtree Creek feeds in river right and just above Poole Road. The added flow and midstream boulder field combine to create a brief but memorable passage for the unsuspecting paddler. Like Ron.

"It all happened so quick," he remembers of the Class II rollercoaster his tipsy sit-on-top sailed through. He remembers thinking his kayaking buddy could have at least mentioned, "Oh, by the way, the bottom of the river will fall out not too long after we put in." He also remembers thinking one other thing, "Wow, that was not really as hard as it looked."

A Favorable Paddling Geography

Geographically, the Carolinas seem designed for the advancing whitewater paddler. At the coast you find miles of marsh, swamp, and slow-moving blackwater creeks. The emphasis is more on aesthetics than adrenaline, the semi-tropical scenery—the ancient cypress draped with Spanish moss, the stark passages through cordgrass over open water—demanding a go-slow ethic. Move into the Piedmont and things begin to pick up. The flow rate increases—the elevation drops 3.5 feet per mile from west to east—creating stretches of Class I and II—and occasionally III—water that elevates the heart rate and tests emerging paddle skills. Move into the mountains and it's a whole new ballgame.

The rugged Blue Ridge Escarpment makes for an emphatic demarcation line when it comes to paddle skills. Suddenly, in the Wilson Creek area, Class III and IV water is the norm, and the occasional Class V rapid lurks around a bouldery bend. Moving into the heart of the Appalachians you find some of the hardest runs around. Not surprising considering the rugged Appalachians exceed 6,000 feet in elevation (North Carolina has 43 peaks exceeding that height), and 2,000-foot-deep gorges are not uncommon. Aiding conditions are the solid crystalline rock that sends water down the already steep hills posthaste. In spots such as the Green River Gorge the drop is so severe that hikers entering the canyon must drop in by anchored ropes.

The region boasts whitewater with a national reputation. The Chattooga, which South Carolina shares with Georgia, is perhaps best known for its starring role in 1972's *Deliverance*, which put a new spin on the concept of a river trip. (Southeastern Expeditions, the Chattooga's oldest rafting company, opened with equipment Warner Brothers used in filming the movie.) North Carolina's Nantahala River is known as much for its frisky Class III Paton's Run and Nantahala Falls (more about the latter in a moment) as it is for the Nantahala Outdoor Center, one of the top training and instructional facilities in the country. And after a good rain, more experienced mountain paddlers waste little time hitting the smaller creeks that offer a narrow window of memorable paddling.

Not all the notable whitewater is confined to the high country. Paddlers in Charlotte have the U.S. National Whitewater Center and the world's largest manmade whitewater river in their backyard. The cement loop, slightly more than a half mile in length, includes up to Class III rapids and runs continuously: when you get to the end, a water escalator whisks you back to the start.

And in Columbia, S.C., lunch breaks for downtown office workers can include a session on the Lower Saluda River's Millrace Rapids, a playboater's playground with up to Class III water that runs smack through the middle of the central business district. (Playboaters are paddlers who like to stay in one place and work a wave or other feature.)

Rating the Rivers

Before we proceed, a quick definition of these water classifications we've been tossing about, excerpted from American Whitewater, a nonprofit advocate for rivers and river safety:

I—Fast moving water with riffles and small waves. Few obstructions, all obvious and easily missed with little training. Risk to swimmers is slight; self-rescue is easy.

II—Straightforward rapids with wide, clear channels which are evident without scouting. Occasional maneuvering may be required, but rocks and medium-sized waves are easily missed by trained paddlers. Swimmers are seldom injured . . .

III—Rapids with moderate, irregular waves which may be difficult to avoid and which can swamp an open canoe. Complex maneuvers in fast current and good boat control in tight passages or around ledges are often required; large waves or strainers may be present but are easily avoided. Strong eddies and powerful current effects can be

The half-mile manmade river at the U.S. National Whitewater Center is great for beginners and, with Class IV water, good for more experienced paddlers as well.

found, particularly on large-volume rivers. Scouting is advisable for inexperienced parties . . .

IV—Intense, powerful but predictable rapids requiring precise boat handling in turbulent water. Depending on the character of the river, it may feature large, unavoidable waves and holes or constricted passages demanding fast maneuvers under pressure. Scouting may be necessary the first time down. Risk of injury to swimmers is moderate to high, and water conditions may make self-rescue difficult. A strong Eskimo roll is highly recommended.

V—Extremely long, obstructed, or very violent rapids which expose a paddler to added risk. Drops may contain large, unavoidable waves and holes or steep, congested chutes with complex, demanding routes. Rapids may continue for long distances between pools, demanding a high level of fitness. What eddies exist may be small, turbulent, or difficult to reach. Scouting is recommended but may be difficult. Swims are dangerous, and rescue is often difficult even for experts. A very reliable Eskimo roll, proper equipment, extensive experience, and practiced rescue skills are essential.

VI—These runs have almost never been attempted and often exemplify the extremes of difficulty, unpredictability and danger. The consequences of errors are very severe and rescue may be impossible.

There may have been a term or two there that you didn't catch.

Strainers: Typically involving low-lying trees along the bank or downed trees trapped against rocks or bridge abutments. Water can get through but a boater can't—a problem in fast-moving water when the pressure of the water pins the boater against the obstruction.

Eddies: Spots where water flows upstream against a rock. Eddies typically make for good rest stops between rapids.

Eskimo roll: The ability to stay in your boat and right yourself when flipped. Keeps you from having to abandon ship then retrieve your gear (hopefully) and regroup on shore. In fast-moving water this is referred to as a combat roll.

Self-rescue: The ability to take care of yourself after an . . . incident. Includes the Eskimo/combat roll and the ability to exit your boat and swim to shore.

Armed with this new knowledge, we return to Ron Wulff.

Paddle Fever

Ron, the avowed whitewater paddler, had an epiphany after his unannounced introduction to whitewater paddling. After getting over his irritation at being naively sucked through the Class II rapid, he realized something surprising: even though he might, at age sixty-five and retired, seem an unlikely whitewater paddler, he was ready—hungry—for more.

"I've got ADD [Attention Deficit Disorder] and that spurt of adrenaline was just what I needed to get going."

He returned to the scene of his conversion a couple times. Then he heard about a trip to the Roanoke River, to a place called Weldon. Weldon is a small town on the Roanoke River in northeast North Carolina. An old mill town, it's best known now as the "Rockfish Capital of the World," the spot where striped bass head upstream from the Atlantic to spawn every spring. It's also the site of the easternmost Class III water in the Carolinas.

It was here that Ron graduated from wannabe whitewater paddler to bona fide whitewater paddler. It was here that he encountered, in the words of American Whitewater, his first "Rapids with moderate, irregular waves which may be difficult to avoid and which can swamp an open canoe."

A curious thing about Class III baptisms: they tend to take place in riparian theaters, in front of crowds. One of the most famous in the Southeast is Nantahala Falls, a two-part drop that, under normal flow, requires a quick turn after the first drop to make the second. But what's really notable about the falls isn't so much the drop itself, but the viewing stand set up river right, where hordes of landlubbers jostle for position on a summer's day to watch the carnage. After executing the drop, the trick is to not get the bow of your boat eaten by the hole at the bottom. If you do get eaten, the next trick is to not get smothered by the raft that inevitably flops over the falls behind you landing square on your upturned boat. Even if you've got a rock solid combat roll, it's hard to pop upright with 1,400 pounds of oblivious rafters on top of you.

There's a similar, though less pronounced situation at Weldon Falls. There's a river access just downstream and some paddlers simply come to play in the waves generated by the falls. And because the access is in a city park, you've got curious passers-by who gather to watch the crazy people in the colorful little boats.

Spectators, however, were the last thing on Ron Wulff's mind as he prepared to go over Weldon Falls.

"The river kinda funnels," he says, describing the approach. "Then it drops five or seven feet. There are only two lines: far right and far, far right. The bottom isn't necessarily tricky, but it can swallow you alive."

He got in his boat, pushed off from shore, and paddled tentatively. While he was visualizing his run he realized his boat had gotten caught up in the current. Showtime, ready or not.

"I was committed. There was terror, my heart was racing, my stomach was in my throat," says Ron. "It was like doing 180 on a country road in my Corvette." Just like on the Neuse, it was over in seconds.

"This time," he says, "I was really hooked."

But not too hooked to realize he'd made some dumb mistakes leading up to this point. For one, he hadn't been wearing a helmet. Had he flipped in this boulder-filled environment he would have undoubtedly smacked his head because when you get tossed out of your boat in a flowing stream, even a moderately flowing stream, you're prone to bounce off whatever comes your way. "I went out after that and didn't buy one helmet, I bought two. One for me and one if someone forgets theirs." Helmets, he realized, are a really good idea for Class II water, a must for Class III and above.

Ron also realized he wasn't in the right boat for Class III water. Sit-on-tops are made for flat water; their flat bottoms make them stable in the water but it also makes them difficult to turn, and that agility is vital for negotiating whitewater. On his next trip to Weldon Ron had a creek boat, a craft whose rounded bottom makes it better designed to handle the quick moves required in whitewater. On the trip after that, he learned it's a good idea to know how to use your equipment. That time, he flipped—and had no idea how to extricate himself from his boat. Whitewater kayaks, including Ron's new creek boat, have a skirt that fits snug over the cockpit and the paddler's midsection, keeping the water out. If you flip and can execute an Eskimo roll, you'll pop up with no water in your boat. If you need an assist to right yourself, same thing—dry boat. If you do need to leave the boat—known as a wet exit—you simply grab the skirt handle at the front of the cockpit and yank. Ron forgot about the handle, in part because he hadn't practiced a wet exit.

"I took a breath of water, then I hit my head on a rock," Ron says. Good thing for the helmet. "Finally, I pushed with all my might with my feet and I popped out."

Yet another lesson was learned on his next trip to Weldon. A paddler showed up alone. He was a little cocky about his skills, a little obnoxious. After a while they noticed he'd drifted off—and was floating upside down downstream, unable to right himself. Another paddler high-tailed it over and helped him out.

Formal Education

Ron knows he's lucky he survived his trial-and-error self-education. He also knows it was an unnecessary risk because formal education is available in numerous ways.

Private outfitters. The Nantahala Outdoor Center offers both two-day and five-day instruction programs. Both cover the basics; the five-day course is intended to graduate a competent mountain paddler. This route is pricey: in 2013, the two-day course was $349, the five-day $749, with all equipment included. The U.S. National Whitewater Center in Charlotte also offers basic instruction for newcomers as well as specific skills courses for advanced paddlers.

Parks & Recreation departments. Various parks and rec programs offer instruction. Raleigh Parks & Recreation, for instance, offers a one-day Intro to Whitewater Kayaking course preparing paddlers for Class I and II water. That class was $75 in 2013. Equipment for these classes is included.

Clubs. I've gone through the Carolina Canoe Club's Beginner Clinic —twice. The clinic is held on a late spring weekend, usually on Fontana Lake (day one) and the Tuckasegee River (day two). Day one acquaints you with your boat and with basic skills on flat water; day two lets you test your newfound skills on moving water. The clinic is set up to give you the basic skills needed to participate in the club's nine-day Week of Rivers event, held over the July 4 weekend.

If you're serious about becoming a whitewater paddler, the latter is an especially good, economical option. Week of Rivers is based out of the Great Smoky Mountain Meadows Campground near Bryson City, centrally located within a two-hour drive of some of the best whitewater in the Southeast: the Nantahala, Pigeon, Tellico, Tuckasegee, Little Tennessee, and Ocoee rivers, to name some of the more prominent. Each day begins with a meeting first thing every morning at which the paddle trips scheduled for that day, and there are lots of them, are announced. Every morning you'll find trips for all levels of paddler led by an experienced club member. Start the week on beginner water and work your way up. No better way to improve than to paddle day after day.

Who knows, one day you may even find yourself at the bottom of the Green River Narrows wrestling with the Gorilla.

Gorilla: The Beast of the East

On a Sunday afternoon in June, a caravan of Asheville Hiking Group members pulled off the narrow shoulder of a gravel country road in Henderson County south of Asheville and disappeared through a narrow gap in the dense forest. The terrain was deceptive: from the road, you'd hardly know that in less than two miles the bottom would suddenly drop out of the earth. Where the gorge gets serious there's a drop of more than 900 vertical feet within less than a third of a mile. On foot, descent into the gorge is aided by a series of climbing ropes anchored to the stoutest trees. It's a challenge to hikers, but to whitewater kayakers the area known as the Green River Narrows is much, much more. In whitewater paddling circles it doesn't get much harder than this.

Through the Narrows' infamous Monster Mile, the river drops 350 feet in that distance and boasts some of the East's most noteworthy rapids: Frankenstein, Boof or Consequence, Nutcracker, Fishtop Falls, and the sphincter-tightening Gorilla. "Gorilla is generally considered the most bodacious rapid ever run by the elite eastern hair-heads," write Bob and David Benner in their *A Canoeing and Kayaking Guide to the Carolinas*, the bible of guidebooks for high-country paddling. "It is a runnable, legitimate Class VI rapid."

Boy howdy is it bodacious. The hikers spent about a half hour on a rock overlooking the Gorilla. Paddlers coming from upstream would pull into an eddy river left, beach their playboats, and walk over to scout the run. Some talked quietly to a fellow paddler. Some simply stared and said nothing. At the Gorilla, the already-constricted Green channels even more, into a four-foot-wide channel that then pours over an eighteen-foot drop. Even successful paddlers disappear for a moment or so after hitting bottom. Several kayakers who had successfully navigated Class IV and V water to get to this point dispensed with

Two kayakers prepare to tackle the Gorilla while a safety boater looks on.

even the pretense of scouting Gorilla and quickly portaged around the beast. Watching the action here in the Green River Narrows was the whitewater kayaking equivalent of catching game seven of the World Series or watching the original Dream Team run the '92 Olympics. They were the best and boldest of the whitewater world.

And for most of the hikers on the rock who also paddled it was more than enough to simply sit, enjoy lunch, and watch.

DETAILS, DETAILS

What you need to know to get started whitewater paddling.

Where do people paddle whitewater in the Carolinas? Obviously, the rivers that offer the most elevation drop are the better venues for whitewater, and you're more likely to find such spots in the mountains. As the Where to Paddle Whitewater section attests, your top bets are the likes of the Nantahala, the Green, the Tuckasegee, the Ocoee, the French Broad, the Pigeon—all in the high country of the Carolinas. Here, you'll find an abundance of Class II and III water as well as top Class IV and V water. But you can also find Class III water in the Piedmont.

How to get started. Get instruction from an American Canoe Association certified instructor. Safety, obviously, is a huge issue with whitewater kayaking, and from that standpoint alone, it's worth your while to get formal instruction. Not everything about paddling is as intuitive as you might think, especially in whitewater. Learning the nuances of various strokes can make a huge difference in your learning curve and, as a result, your immediate crazy fun return on investment. Here's how a typical beginning whitewater class, typically a two-day affair, unfolds.

Day one is spent on flat water, where you'll go over the basics, including the various paddle strokes and safety issues. Of the latter, you'll learn various self- and assisted-rescue techniques. The biggie for most folks is executing the wet exit: that is, when your boat flips and you must, quickly, rip open your spray skirt and squeeze out of the boat (the cockpit of a whitewater kayak is tight, allowing your every body movement to assist in maneuvering the boat). You'll also learn various assisted-rescue techniques, such as using the nose of your paddling buddy's boat to help you right yourself.

On day two, you relocate to moving water. Here, you'll work on the skills you learned on day one, plus get a feel for controlling your boat in moving water—how to ferry across a current, how to surf a wave, how to turn into and pull out of eddies. By the end of day two you should be comfortable on Class II water, ready to try Class III.

Instruction is offered several ways.

1. **Outfitters.** The Nantahala Outdoor Center in western North Carolina is one of the premier instruction centers in the country. They offer both a two-day beginner course, conducted every weekend throughout the summer, and a more intensive five-day course, also offered during the summer. The National Whitewater Center in Charlotte also offers beginner instruction, with various options available.

Get a close-up look at paddlers on the Nantahala River
at the Nantahala Outdoor Center.

2. **Parks and recreation departments.** Larger parks and recreation programs with an adventure component also offer beginner instruction.

3. **Clubs.** One of the big lures of the Carolina Canoe Club, for instance, is its instructional program, which includes a beginner clinic. This two-day program closely mirrors the beginner instruction outlined above, with day one typically taking place on Fontana Lake, day two on a Class I–II stretch of the Tuckasegee River. This option is generally much cheaper than going through an outfitter (see Cost, below), but there is one hitch: You need to supply your own equipment. The problem here: whitewater kayak rentals are hard to find.

Cost. Let's start with instruction. A for-profit outfitter can be pricey. In 2013, for instance, the weekend beginner course offered through the Nantahala Outdoor Center cost $349, the five-day course $749, equipment included for both. The Carolina Canoe Club two-day course is open only to members (membership cost $20 in 2013) for a nominal fee. But again, you need to provide your own equipment. That's for your basic intro instruction.

So, you try it, you like it, you want to become a whitewater kayaker. Here's roughly what you'll expect to pay for the basic equipment new. A playboat will run you $800 to $1,200. Fortunately, that's your biggest expense. You'll also need a paddle ($400 for a top-of-the-line, lightweight carbon model to just over $100 for a serviceable one), spray skirt ($120–$150), helmet ($50), personal flotation device(PFD)/life vest ($75–$150), whistle and nose plugs ($20). Those are the essentials; even scoping around for good deals expect to pay a minimum of $1,200 for new equipment. Keep in mind that you'll likely want a dry bag to keep your essentials (car keys, phone) in as well as weather-specific clothing.

The good news is that there is usually plenty of good used equipment on the market. Newbies get into the sport, buy a boat, paddle it for a season, then discover the boat they *really* want. Thus, there's usually a fair amount of lightly used equipment floating around. Your local paddle club or paddle-related Meetup group, craigslist, and eBay are worth a look. Another option: outfitters and parks and recs who offer instruction typically turn over their fleets after a certain number of seasons. Look for good end-of-season deals on instructional boats.

After you're geared up, the main expense is for gas to get to and from the river, and food and lodging if you are doing a multiple-day trip. A good way to mitigate the latter is to camp.

Related associations and organizations. There are several helpful groups out there, among them:

- **American Canoe Association**, americancanoe.org, 540-907-4460. Nonprofit with emphasis on education and stewardship. Also a good source for finding local paddle clubs.

- **American Whitewater**, americanwhitewater.org, 866-262-8429. Nationally focused nonprofit (based in Cullowhee, N.C.) whose focus is "to conserve and restore America's whitewater resources and to enhance opportunities to enjoy them safely." Also a good source for finding places to paddle.

- **Carolina Canoe Club**, carolinacanoeclub.org. Conducts a range of instructional clinics and sponsors trips throughout the region, among other club-related functions.

Commitment. There's a bit of a comfort curve with whitewater kayaking. The boat is tippy and can seem capricious at first. The cockpit is a tight fit and every movement you make, by design, will affect the boat's actions. Once you get a feel for your relationship with your boat, you'll be able to progress more quickly. And once you establish that relationship, you'll be able to pick up paddling relatively quickly after an extended down spell—to an extent. Read back through the water classifications above and you'll notice that after Class III the water becomes trickier to predict and, thus, paddle. There is no substitute for experience when paddling this kind of water. Thus, while it may be possible to take a two-year hiatus and come back and paddle Class II and III water, do not expect to pick up where you left off in water that's Class IV and above.

Physical and mental demands. Paddling Class IV and up water can be physically demanding: getting your boat to maneuver through big water is a mix of technique and muscle. In Class I–III water, however, it's more about technique, about employing the correct paddle strokes and subtle body movement. Mentally, it's all about focus. You can get flipped even in Class I water if you aren't paying attention; in Class V water you have zero room for daydreaming. Which is not to portray whitewater kayaking as a nonstop stressor. Stretches of flat water and those eddy rest stops give you plenty of opportunity to relax and regroup.

Is it seasonal? Only if the river freezes over. While most people prefer to paddle in warm weather, a hearty breed of whitewater paddler dons drysuit, hood, and gloves and paddles regardless of the weather. Be advised that no matter what the season, some rivers will always run cool: those would be dam-controlled waterways such as the Nantahala River, where the release is from the bottom of the reservoir, where the water is coolest.

Competitive element. There are actual competitions, mostly slalom races and rodeo events, where playboaters do tricks in the waves. Probably the most renowned competition in the Carolinas is the Green River Narrows Race, typically held in the fall on what's generally considered the toughest stretch of whitewater in the region. Yet even this "race" says a good deal about whitewater kayaking: the goal isn't necessarily to win (though any elite paddler would love to break the four-minute barrier), but rather to have a clean run and survive. That said, like most other sports, whitewater paddling is a mix of competitive spirit (*I want to be the first in our group to paddle this Class IV rapid*) vs. supportive community (*Way to go! You're the first in our group to paddle this Class IV rapid!*)

Folks who do this, also tend to . . . do other adrenaline sports, such as mountain biking.

Are the Carolinas a mecca for this activity? The Nantahala Outdoor Center draws paddlers of all ability levels from around the country, in part because of its instruction center, in part because it's located on one popular river (the Nantahala) and within a relatively short distance of more than a dozen more.

Hot spots elsewhere. Up the road in West Virginia you've got some of the best whitewater in the world—at least for twenty-two days every fall. That's when the Summersville Dam draws down its reservoir in anticipation of winter rains, sending a torrent of whitewater down the Gauley River. Twenty-six miles, a drop of more than 650 feet, more than one hundred major rapids, fifty-six of which are Class III or higher. Other popular U.S. destinations include the Salmon River in Idaho, South Fork of the American River in California, Oregon's Rogue River, and the Nolichucky and Ocoee rivers in neighboring Tennessee.

Resources. See related associations and organizations above.

WHERE TO PADDLE WHITEWATER

True, the best whitewater in the Carolinas—indeed, some of the best in the country—is in the high country; your time behind the wheel will be rewarded. But you might also be surprised to find some great whitewater close to the states' population centers. The following rundown of destinations is broken down as such: places to paddle close to

Whitewater paddling sites in the Carolinas

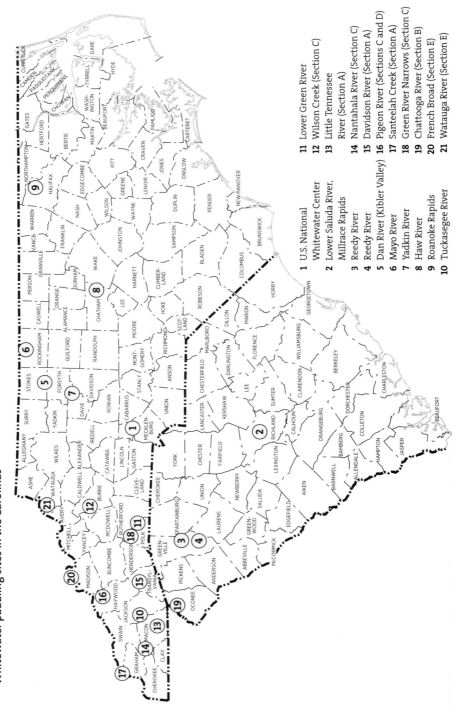

1 U.S. National Whitewater Center
2 Lower Saluda River, Millrace Rapids
3 Reedy River
4 Reedy River
5 Dan River (Kibler Valley)
6 Mayo River
7 Yadkin River
8 Haw River
9 Roanoke Rapids
10 Tuckasegee River
11 Lower Green River
12 Wilson Creek (Section C)
13 Little Tennessee River (Section A)
14 Nantahala River (Section C)
15 Davidson River (Section A)
16 Pigeon River (Sections C and D)
17 Santeelah Creek (Section A)
18 Green River Narrows (Section C)
19 Chattooga River (Section B)
20 French Broad (Section E)
21 Watauga River (Section E)

home (provided your home is in one of the population centers of the Piedmont or Midlands) and top destinations in the mountains, broken down by skill level required.

Close to Home

Keep your skills honed by paddling these rivers near the Carolinas' population centers.

Charlotte

1. U.S. National Whitewater Center. Charlotte residents have the world's biggest manmade whitewater river in their backyard. Class I–III water in a controlled environment. Good conditions for learning or developing paddle skills. A variety of instruction programs are available. Fee if you have your own boat, in 2013, was $25 for a one-day pass, $169 for an annual pass. More info: 704-391-3900; usnwc.org

Columbia

2. Lower Saluda River, Millrace Rapids. On the Lower Saluda, you can put in 10 miles upstream of downtown at the Saluda Shoals Regional Park and enjoy a run of Class I to IV water. Or, if you're short of time and need to work in a run over your lunch hour you can put in at the Riverbanks Zoo and play in the Class II and III water that runs through downtown. More info: American Whitewater, https://www.americanwhitewater.org/content/River/detail/id/1700/

Greenville, S.C.

3. Reedy River (downtown). What is it about urban planning in South Carolina? Are cities required to have whitewater coursing through downtown? For most, the half-mile stretch of Reedy River Falls is spectator sport: the two main runs, Big Brother and Little Brother, are Class V and IV, respectively. But don't feel left out, newbies: upstream near the put-in you'll find a Class I slalom course. More info: American Whitewater, http://www.americanwhitewater.org/content/River/detail/id/3823/

4. Reedy River. Not all of the Reedy River is downtown, nor is it all technical. Drive just 8 miles out of town and you'll find a 2.6-mile stretch, between Log Shoals Road and West Georgia Road rich in Class II+ and III water. You don't get much time to warm up on this run: the Class III Big-S Slide comes in the first tenth of a mile. Note: be careful not to park on private property. More info: American Whitewater, http://www.americanwhitewater.org/content/River/detail/id/3814

Triad

5. Dan River (Kibler Valley). Though not technically in the Carolinas (it's just across the North Carolina line in Virginia) the fact that it's just over an hour from the Triad makes the Kibler Valley portion of the Dan River one of the most popular runs around—especially on Saturdays in July when release from the Pinnacles Hydroelectric Plant above the put-in is guaranteed. More than 8 miles of near-continuous Class II water, with Class IIIs interspersed. More info: *Paddling Eastern North Carolina*, 2nd ed., by Paul Ferguson (Raleigh: Pocosin Press, 2007)

6. Mayo River. Section one of the Mayo is a scaled-down version of its neighbor, the Dan. Here, starting just above the state line in Virginia but finishing in North Carolina, you'll find Class I and II water with one Class III sprinkled in. The river is narrow through this stretch; watch for downed trees. And near the takeout at Mayo Beach keep an eye peeled for swimmers (it's also a popular swimming hole). More info: *Paddling Eastern North Carolina*, by Paul Ferguson

7. Yadkin River. Twenty minutes from downtown Winston-Salem you'll find a great play area just upstream of the Old US 421 Park. An especially good spot to work on moving from eddy to eddy and surfing waves. Just upstream is a 6.8-mile stretch of river—from the Shoals Access of Pilot Mountain State Park to NC 67—with Class I and II water. A dependable stretch with plenty of great scenery thanks to the state park. More info: *Paddling Eastern North Carolina*, by Paul Ferguson

Triangle

8. Haw River. When it rains in the Triangle, local whitewater paddlers head for the Haw River. The 10-mile stretch from the Chicken Bridge Road put-in to the US 64 access includes Class I and II water that makes it popular for instruction and for newly anointed paddlers. The short 1.3 miles from U.S. 64 to where the Haw dissolves into Jordan Lake is popular with more experienced paddlers, a stretch with continuous Class II and III water. More info: *Paddling Eastern North Carolina*, by Paul Ferguson

9. Roanoke Rapids. Lumping Roanoke Rapids (2010 population: 15,754) with the Triangle, let alone the Carolina's population centers, is a stretch, but it's included here because it boasts the easternmost decent whitewater in the Carolinas, and Piedmont paddlers from Raleigh to Greenville find it well worth the drive. The 5.7-mile run is best appreciated for the Class III Weldon Falls rapid near the take-out. The run itself is popular, as are the waves that make this area at River Falls Park popular with playboaters. More info: *Paddling Eastern North Carolina*, by Paul Ferguson

The High Country

Four places where newbies can play, four places that require some skills, four places you may only go to watch.

Beginner Water

10. Tuckasegee River, Dillsboro, N.C. On day one of the Carolina Canoe Club's annual Week of Rivers paddling retreat one of the most popular trips is the Tuckasegee River downstream from Dillsboro. This 5-mile stretch has Class II and III water but seems to paddle easier. A highlight river right is an apparent train wreck; in fact, it's the wreck from *The Fugitive* where Harrison Ford managed to give Tommy Lee Jones the slip. Lots of opportunities to work on beginner boat-handling skills on this wide stretch of mountain river. More info: *A Canoeing & Kayaking Guide to the Carolinas*, 8th ed., by Bob and David Benner (Birmingham: Menasha Ridge Press, 2002)

11. Lower Green River, Saluda, N.C. As mean as the Narrows section of the Green is upstream, the 6-mile Lower Green is civil downstream, especially when it comes to novice paddlers. A mix of Class I and II water, the friendly factor is heightened by a road that parallels the river, making scouting spots that even hint of trouble simple. Next to the Nantahala, this stretch of the Green southeast of Asheville may be the most paddled whitewater in North Carolina. More info: *A Canoeing & Kayaking Guide to the Carolinas*, by Bob and David Benner

12. Wilson Creek (Section C), Mortimer. Wilson Creek, located where the Blue Ridge Escarpment plummets down Grandfather Mountain into the awaiting Piedmont, is best known for its frisky middle section, where Class III-V water abounds. But beginners can cash in on the Wilson Creek cache on Section C, a 5-mile run of Class I and II water. Challenge your newfound skills on Section C, then see how the big guns do it on sections A and D. More info: *A Canoeing & Kayaking Guide to the Carolinas*, by Bob and David Benner

13. Little Tennessee River (Section A), Franklin. A mellow stretch of Class I and II water that's especially so at the beginning. Later, you'll run over a few ledges that will spice up the action. One of the more dependable stretches of high-country whitewater. More info: *A Canoeing & Kayaking Guide to the Carolinas*, by Bob and David Benner

Intermediate Water

14. Nantahala River (Section C), Wesser. Listed first here because this is a popular run that informs the paddler he is no longer a novice —provided he or she runs its 8-mile length and doesn't bail onto US 19, which parallels the stretch. The Class III Patton's Run greets the paddler right off, and there's nonstop action all the way down to Nantahala Falls, about 400 yards above the take-out. At Nantahala Falls, spectators cram an observation deck to watch the fun as kayaks and rafts try to navigate this double drop (emphasis on "try"). More info: *A Canoeing & Kayaking Guide to the Carolinas*, by Bob and David Benner

15. Davidson River (Section A), Brevard. A 3.5-mile run of Class II and III water with several opportunities to practice scouting. Downstream, where the Davidson widens, the river is best known for its fly fishing and tubing. But up here, where the river slides down the Blue Ridge Escarpment, you'll find a scenic, intimate challenge. Selected in part because of its proximity to the Davidson River Campground and the town of Brevard. More info: *A Canoeing & Kayaking Guide to the Carolinas*, by Bob and David Benner

16. Pigeon River (Sections C and D), North Carolina/Tennessee line. A run of Class II–IV rapids are found on this 10-plus-mile stretch of water that flows from North Carolina into Tennessee along I-40. Proximity to the interstate makes for quick, easy shuttles along a stretch of challenging whitewater. And it's just far enough downstream from Canton that you shouldn't catch wind of the massive paper mill operation. More info: *A Canoeing & Kayaking Guide to the Carolinas*, by Bob and David Benner

17. Santeetlah Creek (Section A), Robbinsville. Looking to pad your paddling résumé? This 4.2-mile stretch "has lots of fun, boat-scoutable Class III and easy Class IV water," write the Benners in their *Canoeing & Kayaking Guide to the Carolinas.* "Easy Class IV" is not a phrase you see very often. More info: *A Canoeing & Kayaking Guide to the Carolinas*, by Bob and David Benner

The Big Stuff

18. Green River Narrows (Section C), Tuxedo. This 6.6-mile run contains perhaps the toughest whitewater in the East. A particularly nasty one-mile stretch, known appropriately as the Monster Mile, drops 350 feet, constricts radically and contains such well-respected rapids as Nutcracker, Sunshine, Frankenstein, Boof or Consequence, and the revered Gorilla which, as we noted earlier, "is generally considered the most bodacious rapid ever run by the elite eastern hairheads." More info: *A Canoeing & Kayaking Guide to the Carolinas*, by Bob and David Benner

19. Chattooga River (Section B), Mountain Rest, S.C. Yup, this is the banjo run, the stretch of the Chattooga made famous by *Deliverance*

back in 1972. And it's understandable why this stretch was chosen to represent Burt Reynolds's outrage over a fictional dam proposed for this nonfiction Wild and Scenic River. Lots of drop, lots of Class III and IV water, not to mention the well-respected Bull Sluice rapid. Because of the continuous action on this stretch and because its notoriety attracts lesser-qualified paddlers, the Benners include a more detailed description of this 6-mile run in their *Canoeing & Kayaking Guide to the Carolinas.*

20. French Broad (Section E), Hot Springs. There are seven major rapids on this 7.5-mile stretch of the French Broad between Barnard and Hot Springs. This, combined with an increased gradient and water flow as the river drains the mountains, makes for lots of action, say the Benners. This stretch saves its best for last, the Class V Needle Rock, which, according to the Benners, "consists of three concentric ledges which funnel the river into a giant whirlpool at the bottom." Scout frequently, scout often. And spend some time after taking out in Hot Springs, a true trail town. More info: *A Canoeing & Kayaking Guide to the Carolinas,* by Bob and David Benner

21. Watauga River (Section E), Elizabethton, Tenn. A longtime favorite of hardcore East Coast paddlers, the Watauga River Gorge has lost a little of its luster over the years as more demanding water has been paddled, but it remains a top destination with drops of 200 feet per minute recorded over three separate drops of two-tenths of a mile each. Class V action includes Hydro, Heavy Water, and Watauga Falls. The section begins in Tennessee bit quickly enters North Carolina. More info: *A Canoeing & Kayaking Guide to the Carolinas,* by Bob and David Benner

Scuba Diving

The Graveyard of the Atlantic plays host to some of the best wreck diving in the world.

WHAT IT'S ABOUT

They were gathered in the classroom peppered with posters of exotic scuba locales for a variety of reasons. A woman in her mid-fifties had become smitten by Jacques Cousteau in the fifth grade. A young couple sitting side by side was drawn by their love of adventure (and despite the fact that those adventures frequently wound up with them getting lost). One guy with all the classic underwater phobias wanted to surprise his wife, an avid diver. And there was the young woman whose presence defied explanation: she wasn't into fish; she hated boats; she found the whole thing entirely too expensive. So . . . was it the prospect for adventure?

"I'd be perfectly happy to stay home and read the *Economist* and surf the Internet all the time," Stephanie Browning said of her unlikely presence in a class to earn her open water dive certification. "I'm not adventurous at all."

The disparity in personalities for the diver wannabes among the spring 2012 class for open water certification at Gypsy Divers in Raleigh came as no surprise to Dave Farrar, who has certified more than 4,500 divers since opening shop in 1984.

On the second night of our open water certification class, Farrar addressed our class of eight, which included a range of professionals, most in the tech industry. "You're right down the middle of the road that we certify," he said. "You're curious; you're better educated and driven to learn, which has a lot to do with curiosity. And you're ethical. I've had two bad checks since I went into business in 1984."

Unlike mountain biking or whitewater kayaking or skiing or snowboarding, where a certain adrenal rush is part of the lure, diving at-

Instructor Dennis Zullig sends a student off on a certification dive at Fantasy Lake.

tracts people for a variety of personal, aesthetic, and, in some cases, hard-to-figure reasons.

With Mike Streicker, love was a strong motivator. Streicker is claustrophobic and hydrophobic, two big strikes for a wannabe diver. Yet his wife was an avid diver, and he loves doing things with his wife. So he was willing to take a deep breath—several relaxed, controlled breaths, actually—and tell his wife he was taking an evening class at a local college, when in fact he was sneaking off to the pool to get certified.

Delayed childhood dreams work, too. Nancy Hughes Cowan recalled reading an article about Jacques Cousteau in *National Geographic* as a fifth grader in the 1960s and being hooked. "I wanted so much to be a part of that underwater world," Cowan recalled before class one evening. The fact that she was eight and living in landlocked western Pennsylvania initially thwarted her *Calypso*-inspired ambitions. Family and her work as a chemist in the pharmaceutical industry delayed it a bit longer. But once the nest was empty . . .

As you might expect, a sense of adventure plays a role. Mason

Weems and his wife, Jess, make a habit of taking adventurous vacations. They also make a habit of getting woefully lost. "We were lost on a mountain in France and found a cave that most likely has never seen another human being," Weems recalled. "Then we got lost on a mountain in Colorado and found a bunch of mountain lion tracks." A penchant for getting lost would seem the last thing you'd want when exploring the vast ocean. Guess that depends on your attitude.

"The nice thing about getting lost all the time is that you get used to being lost and it becomes less stressful," says Weems. "After these experiences, getting lost under water doesn't seem like a big deal."

And in the case of Stephanie Browning, who seems averse to even armchair travel, the best explanation for her presence at a Piedmont dive quarry on a July weekend—a weekend that might have been better enjoyed, say, curled up with a latte reading about the latest in astrobiology or the hottest rock stars in microeconomics—may be that often attributed to mountain climbing. Why don a life-support system and plunge into the sometimes-murky depths? Because it's there. "I was never that interested in scuba diving," Browning said before lighting into the various reasons why. But she figured it beat hanging around the hotel while her husband, Josh, who was eager to get certified, went off on dive excursions.

Then again, her motivation may have been what motivates so many Americans these days.

The dive shop was running a half-off Groupon.

Graveyard—and Playground—of the Atlantic

When a Spanish brigantine in a fleet commanded by Lucas Vasquez de Ayllon went down in the Cape Fear region in June of 1526, the crew likely didn't appreciate the fact that they were laying the foundation for a recreational pastime that wouldn't be imaginable for another 400 years. The first-known shipwreck in the "New World" would grow to have plenty of company in an area that would one day become known as the Graveyard of the Atlantic.

According to David Stick, author of *Graveyard of the Atlantic: Shipwrecks of the North Carolina Coast*, the Gulf Stream and its promise of speedy passage to Europe created a lure that made the risky passage up the Carolina coast worth it—most of the time: "the first land jutting out across their path on the run northward was the section of the Carolina outer banks extending like a huge net from the South Carolina border to Cape Hatteras, a long sweeping series of shoal-infested bights and capes and inlets laid out as if by perverted human design to trap the northbound voyager."

From the start those ever-shifting shoals proved a menace for mariners ill-equipped to detect their presence. Travel was further imperiled by tropical storms and hurricanes that would appear out of nowhere—remember, this was long before sophisticated technology that could track the path of a tropical depression weeks in advance—and doom the unsuspecting ships. German U-boats added to the collection of crafts littering the Atlantic seafloor during an especially harrowing period at the start of World War II. During the first six months of 1942 a German initiative known as Operation Drumbeat saw a fleet of U-boats torpedo and sink 397 ships off the Atlantic coast. That six-month stretch accounts for some of most popular wreck dives off the North Carolina coast.

Improvements in sonar and weather forecasting have since dramatically reduced the number of ships going down off the Carolina coast. Today, the main casualties are those offered up intentionally, as part of efforts to create artificial reefs to attract marine life. Still, the number of wrecks estimated in waters off the Carolinas exceeds 2,000. Several dozen of those offer the types of experiences that attract divers from around the world. Their reasons for being and their individual allures are many and varied. For instance, there are those that:

- **Succumbed to the weather.** The *Normannia*, a 312-foot freighter that went down in a gale on January 17, 1924, in 115 feet of water off Hatteras Inlet. Some ninety years later the wreck still yields the occasional artifact.

- **Fell victim to war.** This would include the majority of intermediate and advanced wrecks, including the *Papoose*, a tanker torpedoed by the *U-124* on March 18, 1942, and resting off Cape Lookout in 120 feet of water.

- **Are a complete mystery.** Little, including the name, is known of the so-called "Box Wreck," which rests off Cape Lookout in 110 feet of water. It's estimated to have sunk in the 1930s, though no one is sure of the circumstance. It's thought to be a tow schooner barge (a sailing ship that was demasted and converted to a barge with the move from sail to steam power). Its ownership, its home port, and its shipyard of origin are all unknown.

- **Were sacrificed for recreational purposes.** This category would include some of the more closer-to-shore, shallower, beginner-friendly wrecks. The *Indra*, for instance, a landing craft repair ship six miles off Atlantic Beach in 60 feet of water, sunk intentionally in 1992 to create an artificial reef. As such, it attracts fish for fisherfolks and divers alike.

- **Are popular because of who lives there.** To the uninitiated it may seem counterintuitive, but every diver wants to swim with the sharks. Sand tigers, fearsome looking but generally docile, are the most sought after, and divers find their odds for sightings are best on the likes of the *Proteus* and *Spar*.

- **Might cause the unknowing diver a bout of head scratching.** Coming upon the *Esso Nashville* tanker in 120 feet of water off Hatteras Inlet one might wonder why there's only half a boat, the bow. (The stern didn't sink after being torpedoed by the German *U-124* on March 21, 1942. It was towed back to port and fitted to another ship.)

- **Are on every diver's bucket list.** That would be the *U-352*, sunk on May 9, 1942, by the Coast Guard cutter *Icarus*. The sub is small—218 feet long and just 20 feet wide—but intact, and the water during the prime summer dive season generally has superb visibility: you can typically see anywhere from 50 to more than 100 feet.

A Popular Destination, for Numerous Reasons

In 2012, *Scuba Diving Magazine*'s Reader's Choice Awards named North Carolina the second-best wreck-diving destination in North America —and if you don't own a dry suit, you'd have to hopscotch past number one, the frigid Great Lakes. Which brings up one of the reasons diving off the coast is so popular: warm water.

At least south of Cape Hatteras, where, in the summer, the Gulf

Stream snakes its way up the coast, working its way toward shore. The Gulf Stream not only brings with it warm water—temperatures rise into the low eighties on some wrecks, making a lightweight Farmer John, or "shortie" dive suit feasible. Those warm waters also bring a colorful array of tropical fish from the Caribbean. Cape Hatteras is the point where the Gulf Stream departs from the coast and heads across the Atlantic. Hence, the occasional appearance of a coconut along the Irish coast.

Another reason: clear water. Summertime visibility on offshore wrecks can exceed one hundred feet. Visibility is basically the distance you can see underwater, and while one hundred feet may not seem like much on land, it's a long way under water. Visibility can be affected by numerous factors, but the main ones are weather (a storm can whip up the ocean and everything in it, making for a blurry mess); suspended sand, dirt, mud, or other particles in the water; and suspended organic particles. The latter is more of a problem in fresh water, in the inland lakes and quarries where, when the water heats up, bacteria and algae blooms can flourish.

Access is yet another factor in making the Carolina coast a popular place to dive. Most of the wrecks in the region are found between three and thirty-five miles offshore, making them easy day trips. And with depths rarely exceeding 110 feet, it's possible to get in at least two dives in one day.

And, of course, there are the wrecks, dives so popular it makes no difference that two of the most popular are all but off limits. The USS *Monitor*, a Civil War–era ironclad that went down sixteen miles off the coast of Cape Hatteras on New Year's Eve in 1862 lies at the bottom of the Atlantic in 230 feet of water—a depth off limits to all but the most experienced and equipped divers—and is protected by its National Marine Sanctuary status (the only one of thirteen such sanctuaries protected as a cultural rather than a natural resource).

And there's the *Queen Anne's Revenge*, the flagship of the notorious Edward Teach's fleet. Blackbeard's ship ran aground in 1718 near Beaufort Inlet, its location subsequently lost until 1996. Artifacts from the site have since been recovered and diving in the shallow (about thirty feet), turbid water is restricted to fall field trips run by the North Carolina Department of Cultural Resources.

Getting Certified

So what's it take to be a part of the undersea world of Mike Streicker, Nancy Hughes Cowan, Mason Weems, and, yes, even the reluctant Stephanie Browning?

Although the buddy system—always diving with a partner—is an integral part of scuba diving, this is one sport you shouldn't learn from a buddy. In fact, you can't, unless that buddy is a certified diving instructor. For there's one key element you need to dive that you can't get without your open water certification: air. You'll need to flash the dive shop or boat captain your open water certification card before they'll hand over a couple tanks of air.

Getting your card is neither easy nor cheap (learn more about cost in the Details, Details section). Open water certification requirements vary somewhat by agency but generally involve a couple three-hour classes a week over a three-week period, followed by five certification dives.

Classes are a mix of classroom and hands-on experience in the pool. Some up-front advice: I got certified the first time in the mid-1990s, again in 2012. The first time we spent about 75 percent of our time in the classroom, the remaining 25 percent in the pool. The second time we spent close to 90 percent of our time in the pool. The difference: the first time I got certified the dive shop had to rent pool time at a nearby YMCA. When I got certified in 2012, the dive shop owned an indoor pool. The difference in the two experiences was huge. In the first class our time in the water was rushed; we got in and had maybe two hours to practice our skills. The second time, we were typically in the water by 7:30 P.M. and didn't get out until 11:30 or midnight. Our instructor, Dennis Zullig, would go over the skills for that evening—removing your mask underwater and putting it back on, assisted rescue, swimming through obstacles—let us work on them for a while, then check back and see how we'd progressed. We had lots of homework—online, through Scuba Schools International—but the hands-on pool time was invaluable. By the time our certification dives rolled around, even the hydrophobic, claustrophobic Michael Streicker was comfortable in the water.

All the while we were egged on by Dennis with his tales of the deep. "You see things you can't conceive of," he told us at the start of class one night. "We swim with 12- to 13-foot sharks all the time. They won't bother you." I suspect more than one of us was motivated to get certified just to see if he was right. That motivation is important, by the way, because math is involved in getting certified, and, yes, there will be a test.

The math isn't complicated, but it is crucial. You are, remember, diving with a life-support system that involves lots of numbers: the number of pounds of pressurized air in your tank, your depth, and the length of time you've been underwater, for starters. Bad things happen if you ignore your math. And you must pass both the written test and the practicum—the five certification dives—in order to get certified.

This being, as Dave Farrar pointed out, a smarter-than-average crowd, the math and the written test didn't pose a problem. The practicum, on the other hand . . .

The Final Exam

Diving in a crystal clear swimming pool where the maximum depth is twelve feet takes little getting used to. Most of us are long familiar with pools, associating them with the joys of adolescent summers past. A flooded rock quarry where no one is quite sure of the maximum depth, however, is an acquired taste. While swimming pools are associated with carefree summers, quarries are often associated with that kid three towns over who hopped the barbed-wire fence and was never heard from again. Pools are fun. Quarries are feared. Especially when you get your first look at the one you'll be testing in.

From a distance, Fantasy Lake looks innocent enough. The fifty-acre lake in Rolesville, North Carolina, on the outskirts of the Triangle is rimmed by the rock that didn't get mined before workers inadvertently tapped an underground spring and the hole began to fill—quickly. So quickly that the quarry's operators weren't able to remove the rock crusher that today rests in forty feet of water, water that's surprisingly opaque, you discover at shore's edge. When the water's cold, the underwater visibility can exceed forty feet. But as the days get longer and warmer, algae starts to bloom, reducing visibility to thirty feet, then twenty feet, then ten. In the pool, we could see from end to end.

Local quarries, such as Fantasy Lake in Rolesville, N.C., make great training grounds for Carolina scuba divers.

Now, at the quarry, forever is not quite ten feet. And the class will be put through a variety of maneuvers in this intimidating environment.

"I think it's going to take a little getting used to, to breathe underwater," said Mason Weems after getting geared up.

"I don't think I can do this," Stephanie Browning told Dennis. "I can barely breathe."

Dennis: "Are you feeling stressed?"

Stephanie: "Yes. I keep hearing air coming out of something."

Dennis: "You may have a small leak, but it's not enough to worry about."

Stephanie: "I can't get a good breath."

Dennis: "That's just anxiety. Are you OK, or do you want to take a break?"

The exchange was revelatory. As the other student divers slowly made their way into the water, Stephanie and Josh, her husband, held back. Sally Medling, another instructor assisting on the certification dive, offered to hang back with them. As we slowly descended into the murky green, things were not looking good for Stephanie.

This is where the magic of diving kicks in. For even in the shadowy quarry, where monochromatic bass and brim are the exotic sea life, where an old bus and a small airplane and that long-abandoned rock crusher make poor substitutes for the shipwrecks that lie on the bottom of the Atlantic, the magic of being underwater nevertheless envelops you. Suspended in this foreign world, this world of quiet and grace, it seems natural to suspend your anxiety.

Later, back at the surface, Stephanie recounted the litany of concerns she had going in: that her wet suit was too tight, that her buoyancy compensator (the inflatable vest that helps you go up and down) wasn't inflating, that air was leaking out of . . . somewhere. But then Sally, the assisting instructor, gave her what she needed: a moment to catch her breath, to breathe, to get everything under control. "It gave me the confidence I needed that everything was working OK, and after that I was fine with going down."

So fine that not only did she pass the class, she and Josh booked a dive trip to Roatan off the Honduras coast later that same month.

Which brought to mind something else Gypsy Diver's Dave Farrar told us early on. "Our goal is to get you so excited within a year that this will be you," he said, pointing to a classroom poster of a diver blissfully floating amid a cloud of colorful tropical fish in Caymen Brac.

"We have all the scruples of underwater crack dealers," he grinned. "We want you hooked."

DETAILS, DETAILS

What you need to know to get started scuba diving.

Where do people dive in the Carolinas? The coast off the Carolinas, the famed Graveyard of the Atlantic, is known worldwide for its wreck diving. More than 2,000 wrecks lie off our coast, though only a fraction of those are dived on a regular basis. They range from the famous (the *U-352*, a German U-boat sunk during World War II in one hundred feet of water) to the curious (the *Indra*, sunk as part of the state's artificial-reef program and whose deck is host to an annual underwater bike race every July 4) to the tragic (the SS *John D. Gill*, a tanker on which twenty-three of the crew of forty-two perished when it was torpedoed by the *U-158*). The wrecks generally lie in water thirty to one hundred or more feet deep. Summer diving conditions are particularly good in the area south of Cape Hatteras, where the warm Gulf Stream snuggles up to the coast before heading out to sea. Water temperatures approach eighty degrees, visibility tends to be good, and the colorful tropical fish common to the Gulf of Mexico become common here.

Most of the these wrecks require more advanced dive skills (see the list of destinations, which identifies five wrecks for advanced divers, five for intermediates, and five for beginners). Beginning divers in North Carolina typically get their feet wet in one of numerous abandoned, flooded quarries, including Fantasy Lake in Rolesville, Blue Stone in Thomasville, and the Lake Norman Quarry in Mooresville. In South Carolina, Lake Keowee, Lake Jocassee, and Strom Thurmond Lake as well as the Cooper River are popular inland diving locations.

How to get started. Diving involves surviving in a foreign environment on a life-support system. Thus, it's not something you want to "learn" from a buddy. Nor can you. In order to obtain air tanks at a dive shop—essential for diving—you need open water certification, offered through various agencies at your local dive shop. Certification involves both classroom and pool sessions: a typical class might involve three-hour sessions two evenings a week over a three-week period. The actual certification process involves five dives, often accomplished over a weekend. Open water certification allows a diver to get air (tanks) and go on dives down to sixty feet. Additional certification is available for deep diving, night diving, cave diving, wreck diving, and a variety of other specialized forms of diving.

Cost. This is not a cheap sport. For starters, open water certification runs about $450. That would include instruction, training materials and log book, pool sessions, and the certification dives. It typically also includes the use of scuba equipment, with the exception of mask, snorkel, and fins, which you must buy. That's another $200 or so. Just to get certified, you're already looking at $650. Once you're certified you can rent the scuba-specific equipment: regulator (breathing device), buoyancy converter (the inflatable vest that helps you control your ability to go up and down), wet suit, weights, and dive computer.

But if you plan to dive very much it will pay to have your own setup; even if you scrimp on a dive computer ($400) and go old school with gauges and dive tables, you're looking at an investment approaching $1,000. Then you have the cost of getting to the dive site. A dive boat and air will start at $30 per trip for close-in sites, considerably more for sites thirty miles out. You have to drive to the dock and, since most boats for day trips leave at the crack of dawn, you'll likely want to stay over the night before, so add the cost of a motel room and a couple meals. Be prepared to spend money.

Related associations and organizations. Establishing a solid relationship with your local dive shop is key (see list below). They'll help make sure your equipment is in top working order (this is one activity where you can't afford to scrimp on maintenance). They often sponsor dive trips, and they can help with brushing up on skills before a big dive trip. You'll also want to become familiar with the organization that certifies you. There are two main certification agencies: Scuba Schools International (divessi.com) and PADI (padi.com). These agencies not only offer your open water certification, they also offer certification in various advanced diving disciplines: wreck diving, underwater photography, enriched air and night diving, among others. They can also help you find dive shops around the world, find dive vacation spots, and keep you up to date on developments within the diving community.

Commitment. Because of the cost involved and the time involved, diving tends not to be something most divers do on a weekly or monthly basis. When you do go on a dive trip, however, it's typically for an extended period—a long weekend or a week-long vacation. In such instances, you typically start with an easy entry-level dive to brush up on your skills. Carolina divers also keep up on their skills by visiting the various quarries and lakes where diving is supported. And because of the life-or-death potential of diving, it's not an activity people tend to do on the spur of the moment. A dive trip most often requires planning, preparation, and forethought.

Physical and mental demands. A dive instructor I once knew used to tell his classes, "Folks, I am the laziest man in the world, so if I can do this, you can do this." There's a lot of truth to that statement: if you use your brain, stay calm, and exhibit good technique, diving is not physically demanding. To get certified, you do have to exhibit basic water skills, such as being able to swim fifty yards in a given amount of time and tread water for a specified time. The physical requirements are not beyond the scope of someone in reasonably OK shape. (If you're concerned, ask your instructor beforehand what the specific physical requirements are for the certification you seek.)

Scuba diving is, however, somewhat mentally demanding. Or if not demanding, it certainly requires focus and attention. On a dive, there are numerous things you must constantly be attentive to: the whereabouts of your dive buddy, your downtime (how long you're under water, specifically at your lowest depth), your air, your whereabouts in relation to the anchor line leading up to the dive boat (if you're diving off a boat), the current. Again, this doesn't mean you have to be Mensa material, you just have to pay attention.

Is it seasonal? This depends on two main factors. The first is gear. If you have a dry suit, you can dive year-round off the Carolina coast. Even when the water temperature drops into the forties, you'll be fine. The second factor is your wallet. The waters in the Caribbean are almost always inviting. Otherwise, for warm-blooded divers the dive season off the Carolina coast generally runs from June into early fall.

Competitive element. Only in terms of boasting about what you've seen where. Divers like to talk about the unusual and the exotic. And sharks (even though divers will readily admit that the sand tiger sharks common to wrecks off the Carolina coast are as harmless as puppies).

Folks who do this also tend to . . . This is a different crowd than for most other adventure pursuits. While divers tend to be in good shape, they aren't as likely to be doing other adventure sports.

Are the Carolinas a mecca for this activity? The Graveyard of the Atlantic just off the Carolinas' coast is noted by divers throughout the country and world for its wreck diving.

Hot spots elsewhere. Despite having some of the world's top wreck diving, divers in the Carolinas are more apt to go diving the clear, colorful, calm, and warm waters of the Caribbean. Especially popular are Cayman Brac, Cozumel, and Bonaire. Also popular is Florida, both the Keys and the springs in North Florida. And there's the South Pacific and New Zealand and the Great Barrier Reef, and ...

Resources.

- **North Carolina Wreck Diving** Web site (nc-wreckdiving.com). Great resource for wreck diving off the North Carolina coast. Details on the coast's most popular wrecks, dive conditions, and how to visit the sites.

- **NCDivers.com** (ncdivers.com). Another Web site with information on popular wreck dives off the coast. Also a good place to find a dive shop along the coast.

- *Fifty Places to Dive before You Die*, by Chris Santella (New York: Stewart, Tabori & Chang, 2008). Looking for inspiration to get certified? Vividly illustrated book covers fifty spots worldwide recommended by divers.

- *Guide to Shipwreck Diving: North Carolina*, by Roderick M. Farb (Pisces Books, 1991). For those of you who prefer a book for investigating your wrecks.

- *Graveyard of the Atlantic: Shipwrecks of the North Carolina Coast*, by David Stick (Chapel Hill: University of North Carolina Press, 1989). Additional detail on the wrecks off the North Carolina coast.

- **CoastalScuba.com** (coastalscuba.com). Good source of wrecks off the South Carolina coast.

WHERE TO DIVE

The Graveyard of the Atlantic, a mariner's nightmare until recently, is today a playground for recreational scuba divers. With more than 2,000 wrecks off the Carolina coast, divers of all abilities have a variety of options. And when they can't get to the coast, they've got options inland as well.

Dive locations along and in the Carolinas

1 *Indra*
2 *Stone / Pocahontas / Playa*
3 *Suloide*
4 *Radio Island*
5 *Novelty*
6 *Frederick W. Day*
7 *U-352*
8 *Aeolus*
9 *Hyde*
10 *John D. Gill*
11 *Governor*
12 *Hebe and St. Cathan*
13 *Cassimer*
14 *Papoose*
15 *Naeco*
16 *Normannia*
17 *Blue Stone Dive Resort*
18 *Fantasy Lake Scuba Park*
19 *American Quarry*
20 *James Robertson Quarry*
21 *Lake Norman Quarry*
22 *Cooper River*
23 *Lake Jocassee*
24 *Hot Hole*
25 *Strom Thurmond Lake*

Offshore

Sites suited to the novice diver

1. *Indra*
Landing craft repair ship intentionally sunk in 1992 as part of artificial-reef program
   Dive Depths: 30 to 60 ft.
   Visibility: 20–30 ft.
   Distance offshore: 6 miles (Morehead City)
   What's to see: barracuda, amberjack, toadfish, sea bass, baitfish, and other small fish; flounder at certain times of the year

2. *Stone /Pocahontas /Playa*
Two tugs (the *Stone* and *Pocahontas*) sunk as part of artificial reef program and a dredge (the *Playa*) sunk while being towed in 1931 lie within a few hundred feet of one another.
   Dive depth: 35–60 feet
   Visibility: 20–40 feet
   Distance offshore: 14 miles (Masonboro Inlet)
   What's to see: sand tiger sharks on the *Stone*, wreckage on the *Pocahontas*, lots of bricks and fish at the *Playa*

3. *Suloide*
Freighter sunk in 1943 when it ran aground on the wreckage of the *W. E. Hutton*, a tanker torpedoed a year earlier by the German *U-124*
   Dive depth: 60–65 feet
   Visibility: 20–50 feet
   Distance offshore: 12 miles (Beaufort Inlet [N.C.])
   What's to see: Ship artifacts, spadefish, sea bass, sheepshead, and turtles

4. *Radio Island*
Shore dive between Morehead City and Beaufort
   Dive depth: 0–43 feet
   Visibility: 5–15 feet
   Distance offshore: Shore dive

What's to see: Butterfly fish, sergeant majors, juvenile angelfish in summer; game fish such as sea bass, flounder, sheepshead, and spadefish year-round

5. Novelty

140-foot trawler sunk as part of the artificial-reef program in 1986
Dive depth: 55 feet
Visibility: 10–20 feet
Distance offshore: 3 miles (Atlantic Beach)
What's to see: In addition to the wreck, site includes the center section of the old Morehead/Atlantic Beach Bridge, which was towed here and sunk when the new bridge opened.

6. Frederick W. Day

200-foot wooden schooner sunk in 1914 carrying bags of cement
Dive depth: 40–54 feet
Visibility: 20–30 feet
Distance offshore: Just off Charleston harbor
What's to see: Described in a *USA Today* article as "a very solid 200-foot-long reef wreck."

INTERMEDIATE

More experienced divers, with deep diver and wreck-diving certification, like these wrecks.

7. U-352

One of several German U-boats that terrorized the East Coast during the early days of World War II. Sunk on May 9, 1942, by the U.S. Coast Guard cutter *Icarus*.
Dive depth: 110–115 feet
Visibility: 50–100+ feet
Distance offshore: 35 miles (Morehead City)
What's to see: It's a sunken German U-boat for one. Also attracts lots of small to mid-size marine life—and goodly number of divers.

8. *Aeolus*

450-foot cable repair ship that operated from 1945 to 1985 then was sunk in 1988 as part of North Carolina's artificial-reef program

    Dive depth: 90–110 feet

    Visibility: 40–70 feet

    Distance offshore: offshore Morehead City

    What's to see: Wreck broke into three pieces in 1996 during Hurricane Fran, allowing limited penetration for experienced divers. Popular with sand tiger sharks.

9. *Hyde*

215-foot ocean-going hopper dredge used largely to keep lanes open for Navy traffic. Sunk in 1988 as part of artificial-reef program.

    Dive depth: 55–85 feet

    Visibility: 20–40 feet

    Distance offshore: 18 miles (Masonboro Inlet)

    What's to see: Known for sand tiger sharks. Also attracts nurse sharks, sandbar sharks, turtles, and barracuda. Near the *Markham*, another good intermediate dive.

10. *John D. Gill*

523-foot-long tanker sunk March 13, 1942, by the German U-boat *U-158*

    Dive depth: 75–90 feet

    Visibility: 20–40 feet

    Distance offshore: 25 miles (Masonboro Inlet)

    What's to see: Described by WilmingtonDiving.com as a "monstrous wreck which allows for endless areas to search." Rich in tropical fish and sharks, and the occasional artifact that continues to surface.

11. *Governor*

Exact identity remains unknown, but believed to be a mid-nineteenth-century paddle wheeler.

    Dive depth: 80 feet

    Visibility: 30–35 feet

    Distance offshore: 22 miles (Murrells Inlet)

    What's to see: Not much of the ship remains but the site continues to yield artifacts. Also home to stingrays. Near another good intermediate wreck, the *City of Richmond*.

Only the most experienced divers should explore these wrecks.

12. *Hebe* and *St. Cathan*

Aka the "Twin Cities Wreck," the *Hebe*, a Dutch merchant vessel, and the British sub chaser *St. Cathan* collided and sunk during blackout conditions in 1942. A quarter mile separates them.

Dive depth: 90–110 feet
Visibility: 20–50 feet
Distance offshore: 30 miles (Charleston)
What's to see: Artifacts, tropical and game fish, sand tiger sharks in spring and fall

13. *Cassimer*

Tanker-cum-general cargo carrier was hauling a load of molasses from Cuba to Baltimore when it collided in the fog with the SS *Lara* on February 26, 1942.

Dive depth: 90–115 feet
Visibility: 60 feet or better
Distance offshore: 42 miles (Atlantic)
What's to see: According to nc-wreckdiving.com: "Intact bow and stern with high relief; 3 partially buried square boilers, engine; rudder and propeller; port and starboard anchors and anchor windlass."

14. *Papoose*

Another victim of German U-boat patrols in early 1942, the *Papoose*, a tanker running empty at the time, was sunk on March 18, 1942, by the *U-124*.

Dive depth: 90–120 feet
Visibility: 50–100+ feet
Distance offshore: 30 miles (Oregon Inlet)
What's to see: Large rudder and bow anchor visible. Popular with sand tiger sharks, with sightings of manta rays and jewfish.

15. *Naeco*

428-foot tanker torpedoed by the *U-124* in the early morning hours of March 23, 1942

    Dive depth: 125–145 feet

    Visibility: 60–100+ feet

    Distance offshore: 65 miles (Cape Lookout)

    What's to see: Good exploration of steering quadrant, according to nc-wreckdiving.com, including engines, boilers and deck wall.

16. *Normannia*

312-foot freighter that sunk in 1924 and remains in good condition

    Dive depth: 90–100 feet

    Visibility: 60+ feet

    Distance offshore: 40 miles (Masonboro Inlet)

    What's to see: Wreck itself is in good condition. According to nc-wreckdiving.com: "The bow and stern are relatively intact and provide the greatest relief. The middle section is flat and open." Mix of typical coastal marine life and tropical fish.

Lakes, Quarries, Rivers

When divers in the Carolinas can't get to the coast or the Caribbean, they have a number of nearby lakes and rivers to satisfy their diving itch.

NORTH CAROLINA

17. Blue Stone Dive Resort, 3179 Cunningham Rd, Thomasville. www.bluedolphindive.com, 336-474-0674.

18. Fantasy Lake Scuba Park, 3601 Quarry Road, Wake Forest. www.fantasyscubapark.com, 919-556-1803.

The following three quarries are owned and operated by the Piedmont Dive Rescue Association (www.ncpdra.org/). Membership required to dive.

19. American Quarry, 1020 Dunns Mountain Rd., Salisbury. http://www.ncpdra.org, 704-519-8308.

20. James Robertson Quarry, High Rock School Road, Blanch. http://www.ncpdra.org, 434-728-2286.

21. Lake Norman Quarry, NC 150, Mooresville. http://www.ncpdra.org, 704-608-4342.

SOUTH CAROLINA

22. Cooper River, Charleston. More info: 843-554-0790 (for the Cooper River Marina in Charleston); Lake Diver, www.lakediver.com/cooper-river.html

23. Lake Jocassee, Salem. More info: 803-704-0004; Lake Diver, www.lakediver.com/lake-jocassee.html

24. Hot Hole, Lake Keowee. More info: 864-585-5694 (for the Scuba Shop in nearby Spartanburg); Lake Diver, www.lakediver.com/hot-hole.html,

25. Strom Thurmond Lake, Clarks Hill. More info: 706-737-7900 (for Neptune Dive & Ski in nearby Augusta); Lake Diver, www.lakediver.com/strom-thurmond-lake.html

Sources: Discovery Diving, http://www.discoverydiving.com; http://www.nc-wreckdiving.com; DiveSpots.com; Wilmingtondiving.com; DiveBuddy.com; CoastalScuba.com; NCDivers.com; lakediver.com/South-Carolina.html

Ten More Adventures, in Brief

Whitewater kayaking, flat-water paddling, climbing, scuba diving, mountain biking, backcountry exploration—what more could you possibly want?

How about skiing and snowboarding? Or kiteboarding? Windsurfing? Hang gliding? Stand-up paddleboarding?

The options for adventure in the Carolinas are seemingly endless. This book focuses on six primary activities, but an honest look at the potential here would be incomplete without at least a quick mention of ten more activities. You may look at these additional ten and think, "Well, what about skydiving? Or adventure racing?" For our purposes, we're looking at activities that aren't built around competition (hence, the absence of adventure racing) and that aren't dependent on a motorized vehicle (hence, the absence of sky diving, which is problematic without a plane).

That said, a look now at ten more adventure activities.

WINTER SPORTS

Alpine Skiing and Snowboarding

On the one hand, North Carolina is well below the Mason-Dixon Line. On the other, elevations in the high country top out above 6,000 feet. Geography may not necessarily be on our side, but recreation needn't be left entirely in the hands of Mother Nature, as the snow-making gurus at North Carolina's six ski areas have demonstrated. When temperatures hit freezing, resort operators fire up their state-of-the-art snow guns and can open, in some instances, within twenty-four hours. All North Carolina ski areas rely 100 percent on snowmaking to stay open (though some average as much as eighty inches of natural snowfall per year). There are no ski areas in South Carolina.

Snowboarders take advantage of snowmaking at Beech Mountain.
Sam Dean / samdeanphotography.com.

The skiing here is more extensive than you might imagine. Ski Sugar, for instance, has a 1,200-foot vertical drop—the drop from the top of the highest run to the bottom of the lowest—and its longest run is a mile and a half. Cataloochee Ski Area has a sophisticated snowmaking system that allowed it to open in October in 2012 and stay open upwards of 130 days that season. Appalachian boasts a renowned ski instruction program, while Ski Beech, topping out at 5,506 feet, is the highest ski area on the East Coast. All resorts offer rentals and instruction.

Because of the cost of snowmaking—the highest cost incurred by North Carolina's ski areas—skiing here isn't cheap. Saturday and Sunday lift ticket rates were approaching $70 as of 2012, not a lot less than the lift tickets at western resorts with considerably more terrain. Ski during the week, however, and you can score a lift ticket for nearly half that amount—and you won't have the crowds to contend with, either. Rentals are generally around $20 a day, more for snowboards.

Where to go: Here are snapshots of North Carolina's six ski areas:

- **Appalachian Ski Mountain,** Boone. 12 slopes, 6 lifts, 50 inches average natural snowfall, 365-foot vertical drop. www.appskimtn.com

- **Beech Mountain,** Beech Mountain. 15 slopes, 7 lifts, 80 inches average natural snowfall, 830-foot vertical drop. www.beechmountainresort.com

- **Cataloochee Ski Area,** Maggie Valley. 14 slopes, 5 lifts, 740-foot vertical drop, 40 inches average annual snowfall. cataloochee.com

- **Sugar Mountain,** Sugar Mountain. 20 slopes, 8 lifts, 1,200-foot vertical drop, 78 inches average annual snowfall. www.skisugar.com

- **Ski Sapphire Valley,** Sapphire. 2 slopes, 3 lifts, 200-foot vertical drop, 30 inches average annual snowfall. www.sapphirevalley.com

- **Wolf Ridge Resort,** Mars Hill. 22 slopes, 5 lifts, 700-foot vertical drop, 65 inches average annual snowfall. www.skiwolfridgenc.com

Getting started: North Carolina's resorts couldn't be more beginner-friendly. You'll find good packages on lessons, rental gear, and lift tickets. A package lesson typically lasts an hour; if you're even marginally athletic, you'll pick up the basics quickly—for skiing. Shorter shaped skis have made learning to ski a snap; the learning curve for snowboarding is typically longer.

More info: Check out the latest in ski conditions in the region at Ski Southeast.com.

Cross-Country Skiing

North Carolina has a spotty record when it comes to cross-country skiing. There are no givens in the state; that is, no places such as West Virginia's White Grass touring center, which gets 160 inches of snow

Snow on the Blue Ridge Parkway west of Mount Pisgah. It only takes eight inches of snow to turn the parkway from a scenic highway to a stellar cross-country venue.

a year, enough to warrant fifty kilometers of trail, some of it groomed. At best, North Carolina has Roan Mountain, which gets about one hundred inches (but can be a bear to get to when it does snow); much of the rest of the high country is lucky to get half that much in a season. But on those rare occasions when the minimal six to eight inches fall, it's worth the effort.

Getting started: Next to snow, the big problem with cross-country skiing in North Carolina is equipment. If, for some reason, you have your own, great. Otherwise, the only shop in the state that rents cross-country skis is the Pineola Inn & Ski Shop in Pineola (it's on U.S. 221 south of Blowing Rock). 828-733-4979, www.pineolainn.com. Rentals cost around $20 a day.

Where to go: Old roadbeds (or, in the case of the Blue Ridge Parkway, new ones) make great cross-country ski trails. The minimal canopy allows the snow to reach the surface and pile, and because they are old road beds, chances are the grades aren't severe. Thus, any hiking trail you've hiked that's an old roadbed is likely a good cross-country trail. That said, some suggestions:

- **Moses Cone Memorial Park** With 25 miles of maintained carriage paths, this Blue Ridge Parkway venue is among the state's most popular when there's snow. Popular, too, because even if the parkway is closed (see below), there's access from Bass Lake in Blowing Rock.

- **Blue Ridge Parkway** With a minor exception or two, the 469-mile Blue Ridge Parkway—252 miles of which is in North Carolina—isn't maintained in winter. That means when it snows, the road is closed until the snow melts. And that means some long pulls on the Nordic skis. Check out the National Parks Service Web site for navigational help.

- **Roan Mountain** A favorite of more experienced skiers, in part because of the elevation (Roan tops out at 6,285 feet), in part because of the exposure and views (you can ski atop three balds), in part because of the more intense climbing required. Hit Roan on a good day, though, and it's a memorable experience.

- **Beech Mountain** Beech is known for being the home of the highest downhill ski area in the East, at 5,506 feet. But according to HikeBeechMountain.com, many of the town's hiking trails double nicely as cross-country routes. Topping the list: the 4.5-mile Westerly Hills Trail, which takes in old roadbeds originally "roughed in for development."

- **Boone** If road conditions are dicey and you'd like to avoid as much mountain driving as possible, check out the greenway trail in Boone. It may total just under 4 miles (3.84), but if you've never been on cross-country skis, prepare to have your sense of distance rescaled. (Read: cross-country is a solid full-body workout.)

- **Mount Mitchell State Park / Commissary Ridge Trail** This old roadbed runs just below the crest of the Black Mountains, the highest mountain range on the East Coast. The views of the South Toe River Valley below are stellar. There's just one catch: Mount Mitchell is accessed off the highest section of the Blue Ridge Parkway, a section that is frequently closed due to weather. When there's enough snow to cross-country ski, there's more than enough to close the parkway.

More info: Another challenge of cross-country skiing if you don't live in the mountains is finding out the current conditions. Because there is no organized cross-country ski industry, there is no apparatus for getting daily updates. Your best bet is word-of-mouth passed along by locals who happen to drop by their local outfitter and comment on the conditions. Not very scientific, not especially reliable, but better than nothing. A few numbers to call:

- **Pineola Inn & Ski Shop**, Pineola. 828-733-4979. The aforementioned lone renter of cross-country skis in the state gets reliable feedback during prime conditions.

- **Footsloggers**, Blowing Rock. 828-295-4453. This popular mountain outfitter is a mile from Bass Lake and the Moses Cone trails. More important, the staff is well-connected, gets out a lot, and is eager to share information.

- **Footsloggers**, Boone. 828-262-5111. The Boone store is bigger than its Blowing Rock satellite and has a broader geographic reach.

- **ExploreBooneArea.com**. 828-266-1345. This arm of the Watauga County District Tourism Development Authority promotes the Boone area, and since the Boone area is all about outdoor adventure, it's a primo source of information. Has one of the best rundowns of cross-country venues going.

Snow Tubing

This is the fastest-growing winter sport, at least in the Southeast. You'll find tubing runs at six locations in North Carolina. No skills, training, or special equipment, other than what's provided, needed. Prices start around $20 for a one-hour session.

- **Frozen Falls Tube Park** in Sapphire Sky Valley, Sapphire. 700-foot run with a 60-foot vertical drop. skisapphirevalley.com/Ski_Sapphire_Tube_Park.php

- **Hawksnest Snow Tubing Park**, Seven Devils. 4 separate areas, 20 lanes ranging from 400 to 1,000 feet, 2 carpet lifts. www.hawksnesttubing.com

- **Jonas Ridge Snow Tubing Park**, Jonas Ridge. 6 lanes, carpet lift. www.jonasridgesnowtube.com/

- **Sugar Mountain**, Sugar Mountain. 700-foot-long run with "several chutes," carpet lift. http://www.skisugar.com/tubing/

- **Tube World in the Valley**, at Cataloochee Ski Area, Maggie Valley. 5 lanes, carpet lift. www.cataloochee.com/tubing/index.php

- **Tube Run**, at Wolf Ridge Resort, Mars Hill. 2 runs, carpet lift. http://www.skiwolfridgenc.com/ski_report.php

WATER SPORTS

Stand-Up Paddleboarding

For whatever reason, it took stand-up paddleboarding nearly a half century to make it from Hawaii to the mainland. But now that it's here, it's being embraced like a freshman home for the first time since college. The main reason: it's pretty easy and a lot of fun.

Beginner boards are broad, stable, and buoyant. You generally start out on all fours as you drift away from shore. (Note: your first time will be more memorable if you start on a lake or other flat, relatively still surface.) Some balance is needed to make the transition to standing, but not as much as you might think. From there, grab your paddle and go.

Getting started: Stand-up paddleboarding is done on lakes, rivers, and sounds and in the ocean. Rentals are now available at most coastal out-

Standup paddleboarding in Kitty Hawk, N.C. Photo courtesy Kitty Hawk Kites, Inc.

fitters and an increasing number inland. Rates start around $35 for a two-hour session. Instruction is available and may be helpful on more active water. If you like the sport and decide to get your own board, be prepared for two shocks. First, sticker: Basic boards start around $1,500 new (but should be in good supply used for about half that price). Second, there's the size. These boards are considerably larger than surf boards, generally starting at just over eleven feet in length. A paddle, the only other piece of essential equipment, starts around $150.

Where to go: Odds are you can rent a stand-up paddleboard on a lake near where you live. It's especially popular along the coast, especially on the calmer sounds where beginners can quickly learn the sport. If an outfitter rents kayaks, chances are it also rents stand-up paddleboards.

More info: World Stand Up Paddleboard Association, www.wsupa.us

Windsurfing

Basically, this is a clear, synthetic sail attached to a mast anchored into a kind of surfboard—that's a simplistic explanation, but it gives you an idea. The goal, simply enough, is to let the wind take you where you want it to take you as you navigate chop, waves, and whatever else the water has to throw at you. Though windsurfing is still practiced in the region, kiteboarding has surpassed it in popularity.

Getting started: Take a lesson. This is not one of your more intuitive pursuits, and the time and money invested in a course will help with some of windsurfing's more nuanced moves. Such as just standing up on the board. Basic beginner sessions start around $60 for two hours of instruction. If you decide to get into the sport, expect to spend a minimum of $2,000 on a new board and sail.

Where to go: Windsurfing is done on inland lakes but because it depends on steady wind is more commonly practiced along the coast, in the sounds and on the ocean. North Carolina's Outer Banks is considered one of the top spots in the world for windsurfing.

More info: US Windsurfing, www.uswindsurfing.org

Kiteboarding

You've got a kite, and you've got something resembling a wakeboard. Add some wind and waves and you have a sport that a lot of us will find fascinating to watch but few of us will ever master. One November Saturday in 2012 we came across a flock of kiteboarders (intermingled with a windsurfer or two) taking advantage of prewinter conditions on Cedar Island Bay on the northeast tip of the Cedar Island National Wildlife Refuge. A dozen kiteboarders twenty-five to fifty yards offshore went up the surf and came back down, some catching fifteen or twenty feet of air off the breaking surf. One kiteboarder in particular caught our attention, riding the waves continuously for at least half an hour.

"Kiteboarding is my absolute passion," Michael Schrems said later. "It is an individual sport as well as a group. When everyone else is staying away from the beach, staying indoors looking outside, I am out on the water saying, thank you, thank you for this amazing day!"

Getting started: Take a class, and start with the most entry-level version available. Several years ago I took a half-day lesson and despite stellar conditions and an extremely patient instructor (whom I re-

Kiteboarding, © Intst | Dreamstime.com

warded by ripping his ear stud out when my kite went awry), I never did get my kite up and my body on the board). It's one of those activities you'll know pretty quickly whether you have a knack for. Kitty Hawk Kites on the Outer Banks offers a one-hour Power Kiting course that focuses specifically on getting the kite up, on land ($69 in 2012). If you can get the big kite up and control it, that's a good start.

Where to go: Most popular at the coast. Beginners generally stick to the calm waters of the open sound; more advanced practitioners appreciate the opportunities for air afforded by surf launches.

More info: Kitty Hawk Kites, www.kittyhawk.com/kiteboarding

AIR SPORTS

Hang Gliding

Hang gliding, curiously, reached its peak in this country in the 1970s. It's curious, because the sport has gotten considerably safer since then. Kites back in the day were often homemade affairs, made from patterns found in the back of alternative sports magazines. Today's

Beginners take flight at Jockey's Ridge State Park. Photo courtesy of North Carolina Division of Tourism, Film and Sports Development.

kites are made of lightweight, high-quality material and are well engineered. A close cousin of hang gliding is paragliding, which uses a fabric parachute rather than a rigid wing.

Getting started: Kitty Hawk Kites takes the dauntingness out of learning to hang glide with a three-hour course ($99) on the dunes of Jockey's Ridge State Park. It's the ideal location to learn, with a near-constant breeze (if there's no breeze, the course is postponed until one picks up) and slopes offering some, but not too much, elevation. You learn the basics of how to make the kite go up and, more important, come down. If you're intrigued, graduate to a tandem hang gliding lesson ($149) where you and an instructor are towed behind an ultralight aircraft to 2,000 feet, then set free. The instructor stabilizes the craft, you take over until it's time to land. Then the instructor takes control again.

Where to go: Back in the seventies, hang gliders took off from wherever they could in the mountains. Hiking in the Hickory Nut Gorge area near Lake Lure several years ago I came across an odd configuration of bolts atop a rock outcrop. I later learned it was once a popular take-off area for hang gliders. Today, liability concerns have greatly reduced the options for hang gliding. You'll still find some popular launch venues in the high country, however. Glassy Mountain in Greenville County, S.C., is a popular spot, as is Pinnacle Mountain in Rutherford County and Moore Mountain in Alexander County, N.C. For beginners, the best bet is Jockey's Ridge State Park on the Outer Banks, where eighty-foot dunes offer sufficient elevation for short flights.

More info: Kitty Hawk Kites, www.kittyhawk.com/hang-gliding

Ziplines

One of the fastest-growing forms of outdoor adventure is the zipline. Once the domain of scout and day camps, the zipline has become a mainstream attraction in its own right, with lines popping up throughout the Carolinas. Some lines are simple point-to-point lines: strap yourself into a harness, step off a platform, and whiz to the end of the line at speeds sometimes exceeding fifty miles per hour. Others involve traveling from platform to platform, often in a tree canopy.

At the end of 2012 there were at least eighteen ziplines operating in the Carolinas—make that eighteen zipline operations, because most of those operations include multiple ziplines. For example, Nantahala Gorge Canopy Tours in Bryson City, N.C., operated eleven lines on twenty acres; Big Woods Zipline in Boone, N.C., had twelve ziplines ranging in length from 100 to 800 feet; and the Hawksnest zipline in Seven Devils, N.C., had ten lines with 1.5 miles of cable.

Getting started: No skills required, just a keen trust in a thin cable and your harness.

Where to go: Most ziplines are in the mountains, but several are in the Piedmont of North Carolina as well.

More info: Your best bet for finding a zipline nearby, Ziplinerider.com.

LAND (ON TOP)

Geocaching

With the advent of the personal GPS—global positioning system—in the 1990s came an explosion in geocaching. Geocaching is a form of treasure hunting in which participants use GPS coordinates to locate "treasure," often hidden in wooded areas. Often, the treasures are small trinkets; participants are encouraged to take a trinket and to leave one for subsequent seekers. Though geocaching is generally done with a GPS, some caches also include a set of clues that allow people without a GPS to participate. The sport is especially popular with families.

Getting started: Geocaching.com serves as a clearinghouse of information on the sport, with instruction on everything from how to get started to where to seek caches.

Where to go: Anywhere and everywhere. According to Geocaching.com, there were more than 22,000 caches in North Carolina and nearly 6,500 in South Carolina at the end of 2012.

More info: Geocaching.com.

LAND (BENEATH)

Caving

Spelunking is popular in the Southeast, though most of the more popular destinations are in states surrounding the Carolinas. Linville Caverns is the region's best-known show cavern; you can get a taste of exploring underground here on a guided tour that does not involve squeezing through cracks you wouldn't think a mouse could get through. But that's not really spelunking. Spelunking is about donning old overalls, tennis shoes, and a helmet and following an experienced caver into an underground cavern that isn't lit and doesn't have a gift shop at the far end.

Getting started: Hook up with a local grotto (that's spelunkspeak for caving club). There you'll find experienced cavers eager to share their passion and even more eager to take you on a safe expedition to a beginner-friendly cave. According to the National Speleological Society, there were three grottos in North Carolina and one in South Carolina in 2012. Find a local grotto near you at www.nssio.org.

Where to go: Caves are not only dangerous if you don't know how to safely explore them, they're also very ecologically sensitive. And many are on private property, with access arranged through agreements between local grottos and landowners. For those reasons you'll need to hook up with a local grotto to find out where to go.

More info: Learn more about spelunking and how you can get involved through the National Speleological Society, at nssio.org.

Joe Miller grew up in Colorado but didn't become addicted to outdoor adventure until he moved to North Carolina in 1992. For seventeen years, he wrote about his passion for adventure for the *News & Observer* of Raleigh, featuring endeavors that ranged from winter backpacking in the high country to a Fourth of July bike race on the bottom of the Atlantic Ocean. Today, Joe is an outdoors and fitness writer based in Cary, N.C., where he produces the outdoor recreation blog GetGoingNC.com. He is also the author of *Backpacking North Carolina* and *100 Classic Hikes in North Carolina*. In addition to being a hiker and a backpacker, Joe is an avid cyclist, participating in cross-country and endurance mountain bike races; a skier-turned-snowboarder; a paddler (flat water, mostly); a certified scuba diver; and the owner of a longboard skateboard, which he rides with the utmost respect. In 2009, he rekindled a long-dormant love of running, trading the faster 10Ks of his youth for half marathons and trail running.

Other **Southern Gateways Guides** you might enjoy

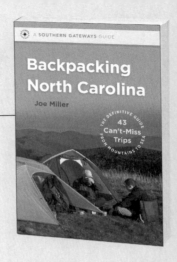

Backpacking North Carolina
The Definitive Guide to 43 Can't-Miss Trips
from Mountains to Sea

JOE MILLER

*From classic mountain trails to little-known gems of
the Piedmont and coastal regions*

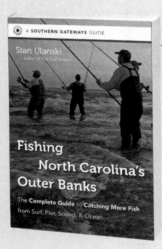

Fishing North Carolina's Outer Banks
The Complete Guide to Catching More Fish from Surf,
Pier, Sound, and Ocean

STAN ULANSKI

*Improve your fishing techniques (and success) by learning the
science of the sea*

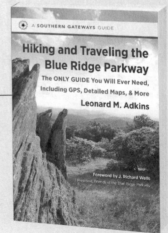

Hiking and Traveling the Blue Ridge Parkway
The Only Guide You Will Ever Need, Including GPS,
Detailed Maps, and More

LEONARD M. ADKINS

The most up-to-date resource for Blue Ridge Parkway travelers